# MOVING
## THE WINDRUSH LEGACY

**The Black Experience in Britain from 1948**

**TONY SEWELL**

Voice Enterprises Ltd

£8·99

T

First published in 1998 by
Voice Enterprises Limited
Nu Vox House,
370 Coldharbour Lane
London SW9 8PL

© Tony Sewell
ISBN 1 872841 00 7
Published by Voice Enterprises Ltd

Designed and typeset by
Aquarium Graphic Design, Chester
and printed by Butler and Tanner Ltd,
Frome, Somerset

Pictures courtesy of:
Hulton Getty
Voice Library
McKenzie Heritage
London Transport Museum

# CONTENTS

For Dad – always be restless – peace is just boring!

## Acknowledgements

I would like to thank Maxine McCalla, Val McCalla and Juliet Edwards for their support with this book. Also a special thanks to Shawn Stipling for his insights. Once again I'm grateful to Angela Hart for her detailed edit. Finally to Adele and Zindzi, whose love and understanding have helped make this journey possible.

# INTRODUCTION

Great expectations and
a sense of vulnerability.
By 1954, when this
picture was taken at
Southampton, around
10,000 West Indians,
mostly from Jamaica,
had responded to the
British Government's
recruitment drive in the
Caribbean.

The story of the people who set sail in 1948 on the ship the SS Windrush from Jamaica to Britain is perhaps more important for its symbolism than a start date of black migration to Britain. Some have compared this to the Mayflower landing in America but the imagery breaks down once you think about the way the black Americans arrived at those shores. However, as a marker to a new modern phase of Caribbean migration to Britain, this was different and Britain would never be the same again.

1948 is an important year in black British history, it marks the coming to Britain of the ship SS Empire Windrush which brought the first of the biggest wave of immigration from the Caribbean to Britain. The period was not only marked by the struggle of Black people to get jobs, but it significantly changed the cultural landscape of Britain.

It must be noted that there were Africans in Britain from Roman Times. We can trace a long history of black settlement in Britain before and after slavery. Nevertheless, the great wave of post-war migration from the Caribbean to the UK can be said to have begun with the fateful voyage of the Windrush. The history of the black diaspora in Britain begins here.

It is the image of the ship, and the idea of an Exodus and journey to a promised land, that has been at the heart of the African experience since slavery. In fact, it is really what has made us into 'modern' people. The experience of being 'restless' with terrible economic and social conditions has not only been the driving force to keep moving, it has also shaped an incredible creative force displayed in the songs of Bob Marley. This creative energy travels to Britain and re-plants itself in the music, churches, writing, survival strategies, humour and general culture of post-1950s Britain.

I have called this book 'Keep on Moving', partly inspired from the single of the 1980s group Soul II Soul. It captures two qualities of the post-Windrush experience. First the idea of a restlessness for a better life, higher standards, rights and conditions. Second, as black sociologist Gilroy (1993) points out, it reflects the newly hybrid or pick and mix form of black identity:

> Their song *'Keep On Moving'* was notable for having been produced in England by the children of Caribbean settlers and then re-mixed in a (Jamaican) dub format in the United States by Teddy Riley, an African-

American. It included segments or samples of music taken from American and Jamaican records by the JBs and Mikey Dread respectively. This formal unity of diverse cultural elements was more than just a powerful symbol. It encapsulated the playful diasporic intimacy that has been a marked feature of transnational black Atlantic creativity. Gilroy (1993) p16

This book looks at three generations but it is really about phases in a cycle of a people who continue to re-invent themselves, drawing on their African and Caribbean traditions in the process. Therefore this book should not be read as a chronological history from 1948 to the present, but rather as a set of common phases that subsequent generations have experienced since the arrival of the Windrush. I call these 'landmarks' the Exodus experience: the arrivant's experience, and the making of a promised land. Each generation has never been static – they had to move through these phases with, pain, love, violence, self-doubt and loss. The important and positive aspect of this movement of 'Jah' people is that it has not only been a physical journey but a psychological and creative one, in which each generation has had to ask searching questions about identity, racism and ethnicity. It has also dramatically changed the landscape of Britain – which was never a neutral or natural entity but was undergoing its own uncertain journey in a post-war world where 'whiteness' and 'Empire' crumbled under the depression. We must always remember that 'white Britain' was never a fixed paradise in terms of identity, before or after the arrival of Caribbean people. Even though some believed in the Caribbean that its streets were paved with gold.

The first phase, the Exodus experience, tells the stories in each generation of 'change' and movement and the reasons behind this. In the case of the Windrush people, I look to the particular history of Jamaica and the wider Caribbean and how that economic and social depression led to the mass movement of black people to Britain.

The second phase I call the arrivants, here I look at the reception that these people received and how they quickly lost the innocence of 'welcome citizens' coming home to the motherland. I particularly concentrate on those workers who went into the Transport services and the women in particular who worked for the Health service.

I have called the third phase the making of the promised land. Here I look at three interpretations of the outcomes for the Windrush generation. First, those who have improved themselves materially and intellectually – some through the success of their children. Second, there is the real contribution to the reconstruction of post-war Britain. Third, is the ability to return back 'home', possibly to a comfortable retirement.

The generations of the seventies and the nineties also have Exodus and Promised land experiences. The first generation moves from being positioned as 'immigrants' with all its negative connotations towards becoming citizens. It is this painful journey through the realisation that although one might be born in Britain, the reality for many was that you were in, but not of, Britain. One is reminded of the National Front racist call: 'There Ain't No Black In the Union Jack'. The Red sea that these pilgrims have to cross is now a psychological one. This is the time of the black power movement in America and the surge of the Rastafarian-led roots reggae in Jamaica – both had a profound influence on black Britain. The building of the promised land is about a mental redemption to Africa and the Caribbean for the children of the Windrush.

At the start of a new millennium, the Exodus experience for those who are in their early twenties is perhaps no different to that of their parents or second generation. The same sense of exclusion dominates the experience of this generation and this is reflected in rates of exclusion from school and the disproportionate amount of African Caribbean young people in prisons and mental institutions. In the case of schools, black boys are six times more likely to be excluded from school compared to their white counterparts.

The making of a promised land is a new process where the connection to new routes becomes more important than finding roots. This new generation has to now build a promised land where they can respect their ancestral backgrounds as well as take their rightful place as key players in the building of a new Britain. The persistence of racism and the institutional exclusion of black people from mainstream life has made this venture a tough one. The world still wants them to abandon their 'blackness' in order to be British. However, the new technological village has begun to see old ideas of 'race' and 'nationality' as the basis of an identity problematic. The journey to new worlds and the fun of creating your own identity has become easier but also more complex. Black people do not see themselves as just 'black' they belong to many other social groups. The Windrush symbolically begins this process and the grandchildren will make their journeys not by the ship but the radio, television, CD and the Internet.

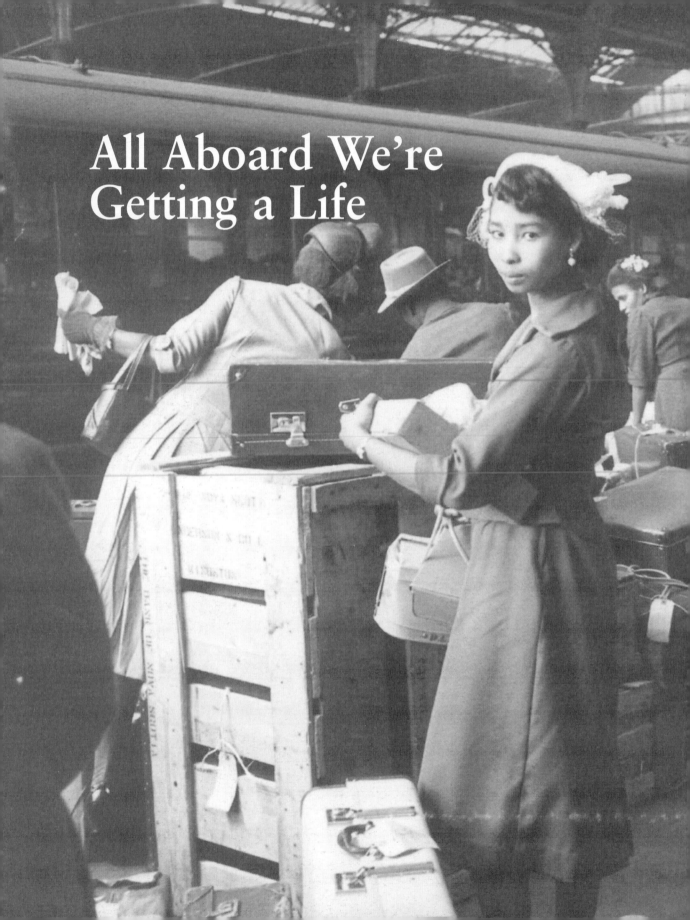

# All Aboard We're Getting a Life

previous page: Women from the Caribbean came later in number. Like the men they sought better conditions.

The new arrivants from the Caribbean answer the cheers from the onlookers on the surrounding launches. It would be a different reception once they landed.

## The Emigrants

*So you have seen them*
*with their cardboard grips,*
*felt hats, rain-*
*cloaks, the women*
*with their plain*
*or purple-tinted*
*coats hiding their fatten-*
*ed hips.*
*These are the Emigrants.*
*On sea-port quays*

*at air-ports*
*anywhere where there is ship*
*or train, swift*
*motor car, or jet*
*to travel faster than the breeze*
*you see them gathered:*
*passports stamped*
*their travel papers wrapped*
*in old disused news-*
*papers: lining their patient queues.*

# ALL ABOARD WE'RE GETTING A LIFE

## EXODUS: The Windrush generation

On Wednesday June 23, 1948 *The Times Uk* reported the arrival of the Windrush under the headline 'Jamaicans arrive to seek work.' The article said:

> 'Of the 492 Jamaicans who arrived at Tilbury on Monday to seek work in this country, 236 were housed last night in Clapham South deep Shelter. The remainder had friends to whom they could go with and prospects of work. The men had arrived at Tilbury in the ex-troopship Empire Windrush. Among them are singers, students, pianists, boxers and a complete dance band. Thirty or forty have already volunteered to work as miners.

This began the biggest movement of Caribbean people to Britain. Technically this was not migration because Caribbean people were still part of a British colony. Black workers came to Britain for three main reasons: (a) The desperate need for Labour shortage, particularly within London Transport and Health Services. World war II left behind a large gap in the labour market. (b) The years of imperial Britain had impoverished most of the British Caribbean: The result was terrible poverty and unemployment. This was not helped by a devastating hurricane in 1944. The hurricane tore Jamaica apart, every parish was hit and thousands were made homeless. The last hurricane was in 1903. The 1944 storm not only destroyed the crop of small farmers but completely flattened the economy of Jamaica. In many ways the hurricane was the final blow for the island and it suffered even more as its best brains and talents sought their fortunes abroad. (c) The third factor was that new immigration laws in America had banned seasonal workers from going there to find jobs.

This was not the first exodus of workers from the Caribbean many had gone to Florida to work as field workers and others had gone to Panama to help build the canal. Therefore migration 'opportunities' to Caribbean people are themselves a mirror reflection of 'migration' requirements of other countries outside of the region seeking to bolster their labour force. The view of Caribbean migration as the movement of labour has informed our perceptions. This is captured in Braithwaite's poem 'The Emigrants'. *(see opposite)*

Another reason for the Exodus can be found in the image of Britain and the way it was embedded in the minds of the Caribbean people as the 'Mother

In the customs hall at Southampton, 1956

below: Waiting for the train. Friends and relatives await new arrivals at Victoria station.

country'. In other words, the rest of the world was on the margins and England was centre-stage. It was also helped through direct advertising and campaigns that persuaded the locals that Britain is a warm and friendly country with plenty of work and lots of opportunities. In 1948, Britain still ruled directly over the Caribbean islands. The largest sugar plantations in Jamaica, Trinidad, Barbados and the rest of the British West Indies were owned by Creole families of English descent. A colony means you live the values of your parent country. This meant that everything that was good, beautiful, intelligent and decent was white and English. Life becomes a sanitised version of British society. The Jamaican newspaper at the time, *The Daily Gleaner* did not see it as problematic to only have white people in their adverts. Even though the country was over 90 per cent black.

Perhaps the most damaging aspect of these 'sugar-factories' was the education system. Pansy Jeffrey, who came to Britain in 1950 from Guyana, says: 'I can tell you the names and dates of every King and Queen of England.' In geography they learnt by heart the mountain ranges and rivers of Britain, they studied Shakespeare and Milton and were made to do Latin grammar; and at the end of the year they took exams set by the school boards of Oxford and

Cambridge. As Baron Baker, the Jamaican who made sure the government helped those on the Windrush, said: 'We were taught at school that we were descended from the primitive and the uncivilised and ungodly until the British arrived and carried us out of the wilderness.'

Jamaican broadcaster George Spence recalls that a key day in the calendar was Empire Day on 24 May. Organisers were sent

# NORTHSIDE HARD HIT BY DEVASTATING STORM

## Several Dead, Thousands Roofless, Crops Ruined

EDWIN CHARLEY'S Fine Old Jamaica RUMS

# The Daily Gleaner.

Price PENNY HALF-PENNY — Vol. CX. No. 170. — Kingston, Jamaica, Tuesday, August 22, 1944 — TWELVE PAGES

ESTABLISHED 1834

**THOUSANDS** of people are homeless, several persons here lost their lives, tens of thousands of acres of rich cultivation have been wiped out—and the worst news may be yet to come concerning Sunday's storm; for some hard-hit sections of the island have not been heard from, Infants, children of school age and adults are finding shelter in Churches and in the homes of neighbours and are already crying out for relief.

## End Of War In Sight, Gen. Montgomery Tells Troops
## New Seine Crossing Increases Threat To Germans

### Destruction In City Wrought By Sunday's Storm

### Allied Flags Reported Flying Over Parts Of Paris; Toulon Entered

### Allied Victory In Normandy Complete, Definite, Decisive

## FRENCH PATRIOTS LIBERATE LARGE PART OF FRANCE

### NAZIS WILL SPARE CITY

### GERMANS BADLY BEATEN

### Churchill Visits Fifth And Eighth Army Fronts

### In Southern France

### Death, Damage, Destruction In St. Mary And Portland

Storm Kills Two In Port Antonio, Two In Port Maria, Wrecks Buildings, Leaves Hundreds Homeless In Both Towns

### PORT ANTONIO

## Fund Opened For Relief Of Island Storm Sufferers

## Stop Press

### "Now We Know" Trial Halted As Blocked Road Keeps R.M. At Home

### Italy Would Like To Get Back Some Lost Colonies

### Russo-Polish Dispute

## Preview Of News In This Morning's London Newspapers

### Reservoir Full: Restrictions Lifted

---

The hurricane of 1944 was one of the worse Jamaicans had witnessed. It completely devastated the crop and left hundreds homeless. This coupled with a massive recession convinced many that their best fortunes lay in Britain.

9

round all schools to conduct rehearsals of patriotic songs such as 'Rule Britannia'. In a conscious attempt to indoctrinate the populace – children were marched down the main road to the town square where they were lectured by white people standing on a platform. The organisers knew how to win the children over, they offered them sweets. As George Spence says: 'I waved my little Union Jack with one hand, took a bite from the chocolates in the other, and naturally enough we became convinced that the Union Jack and good things went together.'

While the West Indian servicemen fought for Queen and country, the economic situation in the Caribbean was bleak. These islands were devastated by the war and the interruption in world trade. In Jamaica unemployment rose to more than 25 per cent of the workforce The average income was £50 per year compared to Britain's £200.

It would be an oversimplification to suggest that those early Caribbean pioneers were conned into coming to Britain. For many there was a sense that the Caribbean was really a world of confinement and that they really wanted a wider range of being. This is seen most powerfully in the poems of James Berry, one of the early arrivants to Britain. A Jamaican and leading poet. In his poem, 'Thoughts Of My Father' he says:

> *Simply it hurts that needing*
> *we offended you*
> *and I Judge you by lack.*
>
> *Playing some well shaped shadow*
> *the sun alone moved,*
> *you wouldn't be mixed with cash*
> *or the world's cunning.*

Here Berry describes through his father the limitation of life in a colony and how passive and static the world appeared. He was desperate for movement and change rather than confinement. He ends the poem with the words:

> *I must assemble material*
> *of my own*
> *for a new history.*

This was another key drive in the minds of the Windrush generation, a simple sense of adventure from the small and often mimicked world of the Caribbean. It is this need to make your own world and create one's own history that is a key factor in the Exodus experience. Berry is interested in being dynamic, he realises that in many ways his colonial past and his experience in Britain has been one of confinement. From slavery right through the Caribbean experience, there has been a real sense of limitation. Berry sees this context as

James Berry OBE, graphically accounts in his poems the limited prospects for the masses living in colonial Jamaica.

tragic. He finds it abhorrent 'Like an earth loving rock'. While all around him the business of time worked on him. The European white was changing history while in the colonies black people were the products rather than the initiator of that process. However, Berry sees himself as arresting time and making time work for him. This would involve leaving home and making history in another land.

Berry came to England in 1948, on the Orbita, the ship which followed the Windrush. In his poems Berry uses the image of his father to powerfully convey how depressing he found village life in Jamaica when he was young. Berry says:

> 'My father in particular was so stuck in the 'plantation mentality' that education for him would have been a waste of time. I began to dread becoming like my father. He became a symbol of why I had to leave Jamaica, he represented the life that I hated. I loved stories but no one was going to buy me a book. He was symbolic of a culture of acceptance.'

Jamaican cane cutters at the turn of the century. For them life had made little progress since emancipation. They lived in a world that still had the same structures of the plantation.

He goes on:

> 'We had no sense of history. I played on the ruins of the old slave mill and didn't know what it was. There was such a strong shame of slavery, there was no process of handing anything down. The world of my father was his machete, his donkey and his land. I had no idea about my ancestors and what happened to them. In school we had no black heroes.'

Berry was desperate to find a new space where he could learn his craft of writing and find a framework to understand his own history. He does not mince his words about the depressed condition of living in post-war Jamaica:

> 'I could see that in my village if there was a ship big enough, everyone would want to get away. There was something about the spirit of the place that had so undermined the people's psychology that they felt they could only make it elsewhere. What I wanted was opportunity, in my village there was no opportunity. People were never going to make it.'

The early poems – collected in berry's first book *Fractured Circles* (1979) – charting the life of West Indian immigrants in the London of the 1950s seems bleak enough; the doors slammed in black faces by affronted white landladies, the hustle for work and warmth, the petty and not so petty racism, and a sense of a betrayal by the colonial 'Mother Country' they are all there. But what his poems of that period also catch, uniquely, is the spirit of adventure and elation that the 'country bwoy', making life in the big city retained, despite all the aggravation. So the 'Migrant in London' declares:

I stan' in the roar, man,
in a dream of wheels
a-vibrate shadows
I feel how wheels hurry in wheels

I whisper, man you mek it.
You arrive.
Then sudden like, quite loud I say
'Then whey you goin' sleep tonight?'

For Berry poetry becomes a kind of redemption for the past:

'I was born in colonial Jamaica. From about ten years old through my school books, through the white family of my village and my own village people – I began to pick up certain established attitudes and beliefs that frightened and troubled me. I more and more understood the heart of it was that I had inherited a slave history and parents and a self that everybody agreed all belonged to life that was irreversibly and unquestionably inferior. This alarmed me. And it has gone on so...So, perhaps, my writing is my struggle, to find, to claim and to celebrate and establish my humanity. But, also, it may well be my kind of knocking on doors for a welcome to a fresh exchange of a two-way reclamation.'

He was able to find a good job and would eventually meet a new group of Caribbean writers based in London. He was the man who would also begin to leave a legacy to future generations by starting poetry workshops. His books have sold worldwide and in 1990 he was awarded the OBE for his contributions to poetry. This is not bad for a Jamaican peasant boy who played on the slave mills and came to Britain to find and tell his story.

## West Indian Servicemen and women

West Indians had served in the First and Second World War and this meant there was already a network of demobbed soldiers and airmen already living in Britain before 1948. There was little, if any, overt racial discrimination in the highly structured military. Outside the barracks, too, the British people, in the midst of war, noticed more the uniform than the colour of the person wearing it. Indeed some black servicemen, on being demobbed, decided to settle down in Britain, especially when they had married British women.

Black soldiers had fought in both world wars and they got little recognition for their efforts. Many on the Windrush were ex-RAF who wanted to live in the country they served during the war.

During the war White women and Black men found love, sex and friendships.

Englishwomen and men from the Caribbean continued their close relations after the war. In many cases, like Alford Garner, settling down and having children.

Alford Gardner was one such person. Born in Jamaica, he joined the RAF after he left school. He said he had 'a cracking time in Britain and particularly with the local women, they just loved us.' When he was demobbed he returned to Jamaica, but found 'not enough jobs, bad pay, tough conditions'. So he left for England, in June 1948, abroad the SS Empire Windrush. So did 491 others with similar backgrounds; and at least half of them had jobs or friends waiting for them in England.

Alford Gardner speaks positively of life on board the Windrush. He had to pay £28 which took care of food and board on the ship. There were only a few women, some of whom had romances with the English sailors. When it came

15

above left: A young Alford Gardner

above right: Alford with his friend's before they were demobbed

left: The Windrush docks in Bermuda on its way to England. It was one of the most racist countries under British rule.

to racism, Gardner says that he got his first real taste of discrimination at the ships docking points in Bermuda and America. He says:

> 'It was when we stopped off in Bermuda that we saw a real colour bar. This was like South Africa, where blacks and whites were told to live separately. I felt sorry for those black women who had befriended the sailors. When they came off ship together, the petty officer told them to go back: 'At once!' in case there was a riot. Bermuda could not tolerate it.'

For Gardner, life on the ships was relaxing, most were young men in their twenties who were looking forward to this new adventure.

Sam King a former Mayor of Southwark who now lives in Bexley and retired as a councillor has become one of the most prominent members of south London's black community since he arrived on the Windrush in 1948. He is

It was after 1948 that the main recruitment drive began in the Caribbean.

now a prominent leader in the Pentecostal Church. He describes the 'Empire Windrush' as 'A little Mayflower' and says 'Caribbean immigration to this country really started with that boat.'

As a pilot in the RAF, like Alford he was stationed in Britain during the war. Arriving as an 18 year old in 1944, he was sent back to Jamaica in 1947 and demobbed. He describes his final exodus from Jamaica, on the Windrush, and the reasons for leaving:

> 'When we got home the economy was still suffering from the hurricane of 1944 which had destroyed most of the banana, coconut and coffee crops. Many of us were unemployed and we decided to take the first ship back to England.

> My family were farmers with a bit of land in Portland, Jamaica, and if I hadn't left I'd be a peasant farmer today. But having been in England and read a few books I decided I could not live in a colony. Everything was done by Westminster through the Governor. Only one man in ten had the vote and 85 per cent of the land belonged to big English landowners.

Charlie Gomm, London Transport Recruitment Officer, signing up staff in the West Indies.

The 'Empire Windrush' dropped off soldiers in Jamaica on its way from Australia to England in May 1948 and we took our chance. There was no regular passenger service at the time.

The fare was £28.10s and my family had to sell three cows to raise the money. To get papers to leave, a Justice of the Peace had to sign to say you were a responsible citizen and the police had to sign to say you were not a trouble maker.

There were about 500 on the ship, about a third were ex-RAF and had some idea of where they were going, most of the others had nowhere to go.

As we got closer to England there was great apprehension in the boat because we knew the authorities did not want us on land. I got two ex-RAF wireless operators to play dominoes outside the radio room on the ship, so they could keep us informed of the messages coming in.

We heard on the BBC news that if there was any disturbances on the immigrant ship, HMS Sheffield would be sent out to turn us back. I saw a man crying over the side because he thought we would be turned round.

We heard there was consternation in Parliament and that newspapers like the *Daily Graphite* and the *Express* were saying we should be turned back. It was a Labour government and the Colonial Secretary, Creech Jones, said: 'These people have British passports and they must be allowed to land.

But then he added: 'There's nothing to worry about because they won't last one winter in England.' It gives me some satisfaction to repeat his words 50 winters later.

On the boat there was sadness about this and there was a move by some activists to protest. But others of us said whatever happens we must show peace and love, nothing should be allowed to go wrong and nothing did go wrong.

Barbados did give their recruits some preparation before sending them away.

So we knew we were not wanted but, being British, once we arrived at Tilbury everything humanly possible was done to help us. For those who had nowhere to go the deep air raid shelter at Clapham Common was made available for accommodation and the authorities helped in finding work. Within three weeks each person had a job.

The future will be good if we go about it carefully. We from the ex-colonies have contributed a lot to the improvement of the British way of life. In 1948 nearly a third of the inner cities were destroyed by bombing – we helped to rebuild it.

Your hospitals needed workers and even today you find our people in your hospitals. Your transport needed moving and we did it. In all walks of life, we the minority people have contributed something. In music our styles have come together to make a new harmonious music.

Attitudes have changed gradually and now we have black MPs in Westminster they will carry on changing. But the black youth have to contribute positively and to do that they have to have knowledge.

I'm asking the youth to seek knowledge if we want a good future. They will still have problems because man is unreasonable. The black man has been climbing the rocky side of the mountain in this country for over 50 years.'

This young woman became a well known face on LT recruitment adverts throughout the Caribbean.

## London transport recruitment: Babylon by bus

In the years after the Second World War, London Transport, like the rest of the country, was rebuilding and planning for the future. There was a shortage of labour across the nation's industries. London Transport simply did not have enough people to do the necessary jobs on the buses and the Underground, particularly those that were poorly paid. Britain was in danger of standing still.

Charlie Gomm, London Transport Recruitment officer, searched high and low for recruits, he even went to Ireland before going further afield. London Transport was the first organisation to recruit staff directly from the Caribbean. In April 1956, London Transport began recruiting staff in Barbados and within 12 years a total of 3,787 Barbadians had been taken on. They were lent their fares to Britain. Even this number was not enough to satisfy demand. Trinidad and Jamaica followed with direct recruitment in 1966. Other major employers, including British Rail and the National Health Service, introduced similar programmes. Although the 1962 Commonwealth Immigration Act restricted the number of people coming to Britain, London Transport's direct recruitment continued until 1970. According to Ken Hunt, who was recruited as a bus driver in 1961:

> 'I came in from cricket on a Saturday night, and on the radio London Transport wanted these people urgently, and I got up on a Monday morning and went and registered...I was in Hackney Garage the following week.'

People came for different reasons. Some wanted to work for London Transport and hoped for quick promotion, some wished to go on to other careers, or to study. Others hoped to earn enough money to send home to their families. Many recruits were well skilled and educated and looked to London Transport to give them a start in Britain. At first the policy was to recruit only single people. In reality, many unmarried couples and single parents had no choice but to leave, against their wishes, their children behind, and families were often painfully split up in the exodus to Britain. According to Esther Daniel who was recruited for canteen work:

> 'My girl was only two years old, and as a mother I was heartbroken...A lot of families did that, because at the time things were hard in Barbados...Well I didn't see my kid till I think she was eleven, because I tried to send for her but the government of Britain wouldn't let her in.'

Many of these workers would long for the life they left behind, although some did use this as a platform for progress. Roel Moseley, a recruit from Barbados, says:

> 'You were not used to sharing five in a room. However poor you were in Barbados you were not used to sharing a room...I cried like a baby the first week I was here. You had to be in work by 6.30 am. If you were

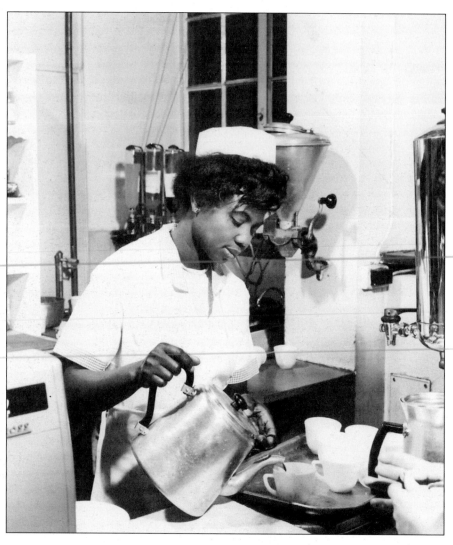

left: 'Tea, please love!' An LT
canteen assistant – keeping
the drivers going with 'a nice
cup of tea'.

right: A platform Guard,
White City Station, 1970. The
dilemma for the ageing
Windrush generation would
be – return to the Caribbean
or stay?

The war had ended and LT were desperate for labour they trawled the Caribbean looking for staff from drivers to canteen workers.

West Indians survived many winters contrary to popular opinion.

late you would be disciplined. There was always the fear of being dismissed. And so far from home, if you weren't working you couldn't pay for your lodgings. You had to keep your dignity. A lot of boys came here and had mental breakdowns because of that stress.'

The exodus experience for those from the Caribbean was a complex one: some came looking for work as they tried to escape the terrible poverty and limited opportunities in Britain's marginalised colonies. Others came looking for adventure and a wider range of being. For many the arrival experience would be a shock as their new hosts became a hostile enemy. However most were philosophical and knew they had to make the best of a difficult situation.

## The arrivants

*'We get the job the white man does not want, the room the white man does not want to live in, the woman he throws out.'* Jonathan Clarke, a Caribbean settler in Birmingham. (1950)

Historian Peter Fryer, recalls how on June 22, 1948 he went to Tilbury docks as a young reporter to see '492 Jamaicans come ashore.' As we know they were not all Jamaicans but his account of their arrival was headlined: 'Five Hundred Pairs of Willing Hands'. He then wrote another story three weeks later entitled: 'The Men from Jamaica are settling Down.' He reported: '76 have gone to work in foundries, 15 on the railways, 15 as farm workers, and ten as electricians. The others have gone into a wide variety of jobs, including clerical work in the Post Office, coach-building and plumbing.'

What is interesting about the Windrush men was really their range of technical skills. These were not a group of road-sweepers, shipped in to clean up the rubble after the war, many of these men were highly skilled, particularly those who had done service in the Royal Airforce.

In terms of the increase in new arrivals Fryer says:

> For five years, despite the demand for their services there was only a trickle of West Indian workers into Britain. In October 1948 the Oribita brought 180 to Liverpool, and three months later 39 Jamaicans, 15 of them were women, arrived at Liverpool in the Reina del Pacifico. Next summer the Georgic brought 253 West Indians to Britain, 45 of them women. A few hundred came in 1950. Larger numbers arrived in the next eight years. Ten years after the Empire Windrush there were about 125,000 West Indians who had come over since the end of the war. Fryer (1984) p372

left: On the Windrush were a number of Jamaica's finest boxers – they had literally come to fight for a living. Few from these six would turn professional.

right: Arrival at Southampton docks – the area still has a thriving black community

Lord Kitchener. One unforgettable image is that of Calyspsonians singing about to disembark and singing to a scrum of reporters about their hopes and expectations of life In Britain. The most famous of these is Lord Kitchener whose real name is Aldwyn Roberts. He was touring in Jamaica and like a number of others from the eastern Caribbean he decided to join the Jamaicans on the Windrush to their new venture to Britain. Originally from Trindad, one of his best known Calypsos was composed on the Windrush 'London is the Place for Me,' speaks of much optimism, ironically he goes back to Trinidad after 10 years. London had clearly lost its charm.

## London is the Place for Me

*London is the place for me, London that lovely city*
*You can go to France or America, India, Asia, or Africa.*
*But you must come back to London city.*
*I said, London is the place for me. London, that lovely city.*
*You can go to France or America, India, Asia or Africa.*
*But you must come back to London city.*

*London is the place for me, London that lovely city*
*You can go to France or America, India, Asia, or Africa.*
*But you must come back to London city.*
*London, that lovely city.*
*You can go to France or America, India, Asia or Africa.*
*But you must come back to London city*

During this time a Conservative health minister by the name of Enoch Powell welcomed Caribbean nurses to Britain. In fact, he actively went out to the Caribbean to beg women to join the new health service. This was before he became their chief persecutor, when he later campaigned for an end to immigration. In terms of settlement the workers from Barbados did have an advantage, their own authorities gave them a handbook (Information Booklet For Intending Emigrants To Britain) which helped prepare them for the British experience. The following is an extract, apart from its patronising tone, it gives a useful insight into cultural differences:

## On the people:

'You will find that the people in the United kingdom are less inclined to join you in conversation than your own people in Barbados. This is not meant to be a slight to you but is merely one of the characteristics of English people. The British are said to be hard to get to know. They like to get things done with the least effort and consider that too much talking is a waste of time. This does not mean that they are unfriendly. If you need help, ask for it and you will find that is readily given.'

## On food:

'The food will be very different from what you get in Barbados. It is not as seasoned or well spiced, and you will probably consider it dull and tasteless. In England your body does not need all the salt which you have to take in the West Indies. You will have great difficulty getting coucou or salt fish so try and eat the English food.'

## On work:

'Remember that ways of life and work are different in different countries. You may, for instance, be asked to do work which in Barbados you would think was beneath you.'

## On cold weather:

'If you arrive in the cold weather you should buy a hot water bottle as soon as possible after arrival. You will find this a source of great comfort.'

## On loyalty to Barbados:

'Whether you are going as a 'sponsored' emigrant, or on your own, **do not let Barbados down**. People in the United Kingdom who see you, will judge us all by you. When you go, you will be getting your chance; many more are waiting for theirs, which will depend very largely on the impression which you make. It all depends on you.'

Most of the settlers were happy at the abundance of work but were frustrated by the colour bar that prevented them getting decent accommodation. This was a shock to the new settlers who now felt like rejected guests. According to Fryer:

Disappointment and disillusionment of many kinds were the everyday experience of the 1950s settlers. It cannot be denied that the West Indians, in particular, had totally unrealistic expectations. The anti-imperialist tradition notwithstanding, their ideas about Britain were largely derived from a colonial education system in which Britain was revered as the 'mother country'. They took their British citizenship seriously, and many regarded themselves not as strangers, but as kinds of Englishmen. Everything taught in school...encouraged this belief. What they found here dismayed and shocked them. Fryer (1984: p375)

Fryer's analysis does disguise the range of experiences that the Windrush generation had to undergo. There were many who did have unrealistic expectations and suffered terrible racism but others suggest the move did eventually bring them a better life with no regrets. According to Walter Lothen of Birmingham:

'Most West Indians worked as labourers, the odd few who had a bit of push and opportunity went further. If you had the aptitude you went to college. I have not been out of work and I cannot say I have gone through any really bad patches in terms of not having any accommodation or not having anything to eat.'

A group of Jamaicans walking. These men look vulnerable in a land that promised much but now begins to appear cold and unfriendly. It is indeed a long way from home.

Walter left his wife, two young children, and his carpentry job in Kingston, Jamaica when he made the voyage in 1954. But he regrets the prevalent idea that Caribbean people were attracted by 'streets paved with gold'. 'I don't like the ideology that people thought England was paved with gold,' he said, 'People did think England was the mother country. When I came here I didn't have a status as a Jamaican. I was British and going to the mother country was like going from one parish to another. You had no conception of it being different.'

But he said: 'Everything was different. The climate was different. You had to have time to adapt. Living conditions were deplorable.' He did not lose heart,

# The Daily Gleaner.

LARGEST CIRCULATION    ESTABLISHED 1834    Price: TWOPENCE

Vol. CXIV No. 147.    KINGSTON, JAMAICA, WEDNESDAY, JUNE 23, 1948.    SIXTEEN PAGES

**West Indians arrive in U.K.**
**in search of jobs**

**Hill statement is**
**officially denied**

**Bustamante given**
**big send - off**

# NEW LIFE IN SOMBRE SETTING
# FOR W.I. JOB-SEEKERS

*'What do British*
*people think of*
*our coming here?'*

(Special cable to the "Gleaner" from our London correspondent).
(Gleaner copyright, 1948)

LONDON, June 22.—Under grey skies, and borne on the broad bosom of London's river, 400 West Indians entered a new world today—though their new world was the old world of the history books.

As I watched the troopship "Empire Windrush," with West Indians crowding the rails, edging into the Tilbury quayside at seven o'clock this morning, I thought of all the voyagers who had sailed from Britain across the Atlantic in search of fortune. There was romance in this "Westward Ho" in reverse.

### Matter-of-Fact

But none of the West Indian boys in search of jobs seemed to feel any touch of romance. On the crowded deck of the "Empire Windrush," I found them surprisingly matter-of-fact and prepared to take everything as it came.

Even their natural curiosity to the Thames and the smoke of London in the distance, had begun to wear off since their 14,000 ton ship anchored in the stream last night. It required a sight of the morning papers with the printed references to their arrival before they began to talk and evinced any marked interest in themselves.

Then the question was: "What do the British people think of our coming here?" My reassuring replies were taken quietly, continuously—and sensible well-informed comments on the bearing shortage here, and the prospects of jobs, showed that they realised that the going at first might be tough.

The arrival, biggest wave so far of an "emigration in reverse" by renowned British subjects from the West Indies and West Africa included singers students pianists and a complete swing band. (Detroy Stephens and his "Commandos" from Jamaica), as well as former Royal Air Force men.

### Temporary Offices

As the men queued up for breakfast, each with a large mug of his hand, a regiment of Ministry of Labour and Colonial officials were boarding the ship and setting up *(Continued on page 9)*

## The Lucky Woman Stowaway

(Special Cable to Gleaner from our Correspondent)

LONDON, June 22.—Luckiest West Indian on board the Empire Windrush was 25-year-old Averill Wauchope, a dressmaker from Kingston, who was one of six stowaways on board.

When discovered a week out of Kingston she was befriended by Miss Nancy Cunard, heiress of the Cunard fortunes, and Mortimer Martin, bottling manager, who was a passenger, organised a subscription which raised £50 for her fare and left £6 for her expenses on arrival here.

Five stowaways are expected to be prosecuted in the Tilbury Police Court. Two others were put off at Bermuda.

## Chief Dispenser To Retire From Service

Mr. Egbert B. Bryce, chief dispenser at the Kingston Public Hospital, has gone on 6 months leave of absence prior to retiring from the Government Medical Service.

Mr. Bryce has been in the service for over 30 years. He was trained at the Kingston Public Hospital by the late Mr. R. N. Gordon.

THE DAILY MAIL, Tuesday, June 22, 1948.    3

**MINUTE MAIL**

### 492 IMMIGRANTS IN SEARCH OF A JOB

# Cheers for men from Jamaica

AS darkness fell at Tilbury last night launches crowded with sightseers were still circling the ex-troopship Empire Windrush, which has brought 492 Jamaicans to look for work in Britain.

The people aboard the launches shouted and waved greetings, and the Jamaicans climbed the rails to wave and shout back.

Early today the Empire Windrush will pull into the landing stage and the Jamaicans will disembark.

Colonial Office officials went to meet the men in this biggest "emmigration-in-reverse" operation.

Fifty-two of the Jamaicans will volunteer for the R.A.F. or the Army; 204 have friends who can give them a prospect of employment; 236 are without jobs.

These 236 will stay in Clapham Common deep shelter where they will be interviewed by the Ministry of Labour.

Contrasting messages. The Daily Gleaner has a more pessimistic outlook for the new arrivants. While London, Daily Mail is euphoric about the help from the Caribbean.

# The Daily Gleaner

LARGEST CIRCULATION    ESTABLISHED 1834    Price: TWOPENCE

Vol. CXIV No. 137.    KINGSTON, JAMAICA. WEDNESDAY, JUNE 9, 1948.    EIGHTEEN PAGES

*'No assurance that they can be found suitable work'*

# JAMAICANS ON WAY TO U.K. FACE DISAPPOINTMENTS

## Minister of Labour gives warning in Commons

LONDON, June 8.—(Reuter).—The Minister of Labour, George Isaacs, warned today that "considerable difficulties and disappointment" await 500 West Indians now on the high seas headed for Britain to look for jobs.

The West Indians coming from the British Colonies of Jamiaca and Trinidad are travelling in the 14,000-ton vessel "Empire Windrush," due in London on June 19.

Mr. Isaacs, who was replying to a question in the House of Commons, said the West Indians would be met and told how to register for employment but, he added: "The arrival of this substantial number of men under the present housing shortage is going to cause considerable difficulties and disappointment. I have no knowledge of their qualifications or capacity and can give no assurance that they can be found suitable work."

An official of the Colonial Office said most of the immigrants were technicians, including radio engineers, electricians and major mechanics who had learned their trade while serving in the British Forces. They were paying for their passage and and would be met by welfare officers to help them find accommodation and work.

This will be the biggest wave yet in an "immigration in reverse" movement from the West Indies and West Africa to Britain that has been going on since the end of the war, while there are thousands of Britons who are eager to immigrate to Australia, South Africa, Canada and other countries.

Many British subjects have made their way here as stowaways and have found England a haven for employment they could not find at home.

Mr. Isaacs said he did not know who was responsible for the trip of the West Indians who as British subjects, cannot be prevented from landing.

# The Daily Gleaner.

LARGEST CIRCULATION    ESTABLISHED 1834    Price: TWOPENCE

Vol. CXIV No. 147.    KINGSTON, JAMAICA, WEDNESDAY, JUNE 23, 1948.    SIXTEEN PAGES

*West Indians arrive in U.K. in search of jobs*    *Hill statement is officially denied*    *Bustamante given big send-off*

# NEW LIFE IN SOMBRE SETTING FOR W.I. JOB-SEEKERS

## 'What do British people think of our coming here?'

(Special cable to the "Gleaner" from our London correspondent).
(Gleaner copyright, 1948)

LONDON, June 22.—Under grey skies, and borne on the broad bosom of London's river, 400 West Indians entered a new world today—though their new world was the old world of the history books.

As I watched the troopship "Empire Windrush," with West Indians crowding the rails, edging into the Tilbury quayside at seven o'clock this morning, I thought of all the voyagers who had sailed from Britain across the Atlantic in search of fortune. There was romance in this "Westward Ho" in reverse.

### The Lucky Woman Stowaway

(Special Cable to Gleaner from our Correspondent)

LONDON, June 22.—Luckiest West Indian on board the Empire Windrush was 25-year-old Averill Wauchope, a dress-maker from Kingston, who was one of six stowaways on board.

When discovered a week out of Kingston she was befriended by Miss Nancy Cunard, heiress of the Cunard fortune, and Mr. Peter Martin, hotting manager, who was a passenger, organised a subscription which paid her life fare and half-fare for her next meals on arrival here.

The stowaways are expected to be presented in the Tilbury Police Court. They return were picked up across on arrival here.

### Chief Dispenser To Retire From Service

Mr. Edwin E. Bryce, chief dispenser at the Kingston Public Hospital, has gone on 6 months leave of absence prior to retiring from the Government Medical Service.

Mr. Bryce has been in the service for over 30 years. He was trained at the Kingston Public Hospital by the late R. N. Gordon.

### Matter-of-Fact

But none of the West Indian boys in search of jobs seemed to feel any touch of romance. On the crowded deck of the "Empire Windrush," I found them supremely matter-of-fact and prepared to take everything as it came.

Even their natural curiosity in the Thames and the shipping and the smoke of London in the distance had begun to wear off since their 14,000 ton ship anchored in the stream last night. It required a sight of the morning papers with the printed references to their arrival before they began to talk and evinced any marked interest in themselves.

Then the question was: "What do the British people think of our coming here?" My reassuring replies were taken gravely, occasionally and optimistic when informed permanents at the boarding sheetings here, and the prospects of them showed that they realised that the going at first might be tough.

The arrival's biggest hero so far is not emigration in reverse by nation of these nochers. There are in the east West Africa including a complete swing band (Dairily Engleton and his "Commandos" from Jamaica), as well as former Royal Air Force men.

### Temporary Offices

As the men queued up for breakfast, each with a large mug till his hand, a regiment of Ministry of Labour and Colonial officials were boarding the ship, and setting up

(Continued on page 8)

The Daily Gleaner seems to have never liked the idea that the best skills of the island were going to Britain. It doesn't even wish the new migrants well.

During the fifties, there was little prospect of finding decent accommodation. There was even less sympathy if you had children.

and went to college to study engineering: 'I became a machine toolsetter and since then I worked in two jobs.' If jobs were not a big problem for Walter, accommodation was:

> '...appalling. A lot of landlords didn't want to know you. Half the houses had no bath. You had one toilet for five or six houses and had to go to the public baths. The landlords used to search the rooms when we were at work and often our property went missing.'

In the context of these harsh conditions, Walter is philosophical he made the best of his situation irrespective of the hardships and, unlike others, he didn't want to go back home. He saved up and brought his own home in Small Heath, Birmingham, in 1957. His wife and children then followed him over to England.

Horace Ove, from Trinidad, was not from a poor background and came to Britain to study design. He got a rude awakening. He has since gone on to be one of Britain's leading filmmakers.

There was a huge gap between expectations and reality. This was the case for Trinidadian photographer and film-maker Horace Ove:

> 'When I left the Caribbean I felt I was coming to a paradise, like Alice in Wonderland,' recalls Ove who came to Britain in the late 1950s. But when Ove passed through Customs he found a world quite divorced from his expectations. He was shocked at how grubby and depressed the streets and people looked. This was the downcast fifties, where everyone was dressed in black and grey as if they were going to a funeral. 'Then it suddenly hit me what I had left behind and where I had come to.'

Ove was also surprised when he heard a taxi-driver's cockney accent. 'I couldn't understand a damn word when the cabby started speaking to me. In the Caribbean I had only had contact with gentlemen and the upper classes.' Like many others he was surprised at seeing white manual labourers. In the Caribbean menial work was performed exclusively by Black and Asian people.

Ove represents a professional and skilled class of people who made the journey. This counters the myth that those who left were unskilled labourers. In 1958 the Earl of Swinton told the House of Lords that the great majority of West Indians coming to Britain were unskilled. Or as a local London newspaper put it, England was becoming the 'dumping ground for the world's riff-raff.'

The statistics tell another story, 24 per cent of the West Indians coming to Britain had professional or managerial experience, 46 per cent were skilled workers, 5 per cent semi-skilled and only 13 per cent unskilled manual workers. According to Pilkington (1988):

> A very wide range of professions were reflected among the passengers on board the Empire Windrush: masons, mechanics, journalists, students, musicians, boxers and even cyclists attending an international competition. Many of the ex-servicemen who returned to Britain had spent five years in the RAF learning and practising skills that would have equipped them for virtually any job in mechanics on the market. Moreover, most were in their twenties, and they all spoke English. Indeed, the West Indies were losing some of the cream of their labour force. Pilkington (1988)

No room in the Inn. A black man walks the streets of London still hoping for that kind landlady.

What was frustrating for the skilled and professional workers was the lack of opportunities because they were black. Horace Ove was hoping to study interior design with a firm of architects, he had all the right credentials. But when he arrived at a recommended firm in London he was told: 'We don't employ people like you.' In a country which at this time had no anti-racist legislation, Ove was deeply disappointed: 'That was my first experience of racism in Britain.'

The Atlee Government appeared unperturbed by the influx of West Indians and ministers made no public comment on the matter. Indeed, there seemed no reason why they should. The arrivants from the Caribbean came of their own free will, paid their own passage, found their own accommodation and jobs and didn't make any trouble. The policy was a lazy one in which the desperate need for Labour made this insular country open its gates to its colonies in the Caribbean.

However there was an internal war in government between the Ministry Of Labour and the Colonial Office. Those responsible for colonies were concerned about unemployment and potential unrest in the West Indies, they saw migration to Britain as a solution – any restriction would cause unrest in the colonies. The Ministry of Labour was concerned about the political effects of immigration to Britain and whether this new influx would cause un-employment.

It was becoming increasingly evident in the 1950s that the British Government in Westminster and the colonial governments abroad were at loggerheads. The main reason was that secretly the British government, devastated by war, could see little benefits in keeping these ailing economies afloat. They were a massive burden on the economy. The Caribbean economy remained almost completely undeveloped. The traditional sugar crop, still accounted for over half of the total produce of the West Indies and 90 per cent of Barbados exports. Inflation and unemployment soared and the hurricane in Jamaica in 1944 added to the devastation of that economy. Ironically, Britain, having begun her colonisation of the West Indies by forcing black people to work as slaves, ended it leaving thousands of these people without any work.

There was another important reason why the Ministry of Labour was not enthusiastic about importing black workers in the early 1950s, this was

right: A letter back home perhaps? Men in the Clapham Air Raid Shelter – taking cover from racism.

below: Jobs were abundant but what about a managerial post!

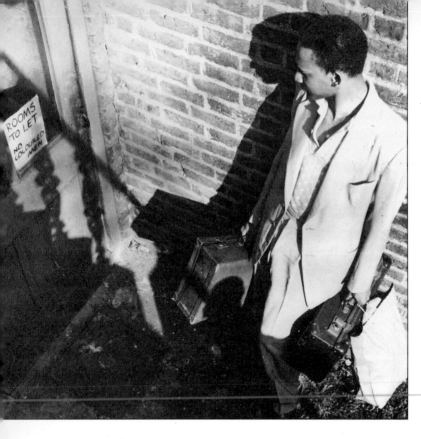

Welcome to the Motherland! The sign says 'No Coloured men.' The accommodation situation was so bad that many people ended up in hostels.

because of the new immigration laws. Until 1948 West Indians, although technically British subjects, were restricted in their entry to Britain. This was removed in the Nationality Acts of that year which gave all Commonwealth and Colonies people a right to live and work in Britain. This gave them little or no control over the movement of black labour.

Faced with the choice between having European labour or continuing with the policy of using West Indians, the Ministry of Labour opted for Europeans.

It was only when the pressure began to bite due to the chronic Labour shortage that the government abandoned its plans of cutting black Immigration. Therefore in 1956 London Transport and later the health service began their recruitment campaign in the Caribbean.

Attitudes again changed when Britain had another bout of unemployment. By 1958 half a million people were jobless – a little over 2 per cent of the workforce. As employers such as London Transport began to cut jobs, the black workers were blamed for taking white jobs and diluting skills and pay. It would be at these times of economic crisis that the racism against black people would intensify. In the case of London Transport white men threatened to withdraw their wives from the buses, saying they did not know what to think when their wives worked late with black men. 'We are much more selective now,' said a London Transport recruiting officer, 'although there was a time when we were glad to take anybody. LT. used to be called Jamaica Inn. But not now.'

## Two Windrush stories

### Edwin Ho: The man in search of adventure

Most people think that the Windrush was only occupied by Jamaicans. In fact there were approximately 100 of the 492 who were from other Caribbean islands. Henry Ho was from Guyana – a chef, a fly-weight boxer and racially a mixture of Indian, black and Chinese. He was a man that no one could miss. Just before his departure on the Windrush, he had adventures in the Caribbean which would dramatically change his life, he says: 'I was suppose to be in the RAF but I missed the boat. During the war, I did my home service in Guyana. I was a rebel as a boy and, although my father was one of the richest men in Guyana, I did not want to work in the family Timber business. I decided to go to Brazil on an adventure. I worked for a mining company which I soon left and began a trek through the jungle for four days and four nights – I came to the coast and got a boat back to Georgetown.'

After getting several jobs on cargo ships. Empire Windrush was now docked in Trinidad:

> 'I was in Guyana at the time and there was a leaflet and poster campaign, which quoted the British Prime Minister. It was saying that we need you to come and re-build the mother country. The fare was £28, once we made our way to Trinidad. It was after Trinidad that we went to Jamaica.'

So why did Edwin Ho want to come to England?

> 'One of the reasons for my desire to travel was that I didn't want to be under my parent's footsteps, I wanted to make my own way in life. Another reason for going was that I was about to get married and in a heavy night of gambling I lost all our savings of around 35,000 dollars.' His wife left him but she did turn up to see him off. He needed to escape the confinement of his parents at Guyana.'

What was life like on the boat:

> 'The trip was fantastic, we made our own entertainment. There was a call for any boxers to take part in a match. I was a champion back in Guyana. So naturally I went forward. I was up against the Jamaican bantam weight champion. Even though he had fanatical support from the Jamaicans on deck, I knocked him out in the third round. I was approached by a promoter who said I should come to Liverpool to fight for him, but I declined the offer.'

Eddie Ho goes on to talk about life in England in those early days:

Mostly Jamaican arrivants collect a meal from the canteen set for them at a hostel in the Clapham air raid shelter, south London.

'When we arrived at Tilbury docks they took all those who didn't have any friends or relatives in England. They gave us £5 each. They took us by coaches down to Clapham Common and to the converted Air-raid Shelter. Across the road was a big park with tents. You go there and have your meal – they gave you a ticket.'

It wasn't long before the name of Henry Ho was heard over the loud speakers, someone had come to see him:

'I was called to see boxing promoters Jack Solomon and Ted Lewis. They showed me a picture of me boxing on the Windrush. It was in the *Daily Express*. I and two other boxers were wined and dined. We worked out well in the ring and were each given a goodwill fee of £5 each, on the understanding that we signed up later. We decided to do a runner and find jobs. I got a job in a foundry in Telford. To this day I regret the decision.'

A postcard picture of the Windrush – lovingly kept by Edwin Ho.

below: Looking cool! Edwin Ho – the man who gambled away his wedding money and then took flight on the Windrush

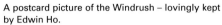

above right: Edwin Ho was a champion boxer in Guyana and he needed his skills on the streets of Britain.

below: Edwin Ho today at 80, now lives in Birmingham.

In order to supplement his poultry sum of £7 a week, he did unlicensed boxing. This took off really well and he would travel around the country knocking out the best man in town. Life was not always positive, he experienced many racist attacks on the streets:

> 'When I was coming home from work I had no ends of fights with these white people. I could fight in those days and so I wouldn't stand for it. I remember going to a dance and my friend from the Windrush was dancing with a white woman. He was dragged away by a white man – all hell broke loose and the fighting spilled out onto the streets. I was chased by a whole gang and I saw a river-bank so that no one could come from behind. During the attack I managed to knockout three of them. They still arrested me and I was ordered to pay 10 shillings.'

Do you feel it was worth while?

> 'I have no regrets about coming to England. I got married to a lovely Austrian woman and I have three children who have done very well but they had to move to Canada to fulfil their ambitions. It was only those early days where I found life hard. Work was plentiful but the people never liked us.'

## Vince Reid: The Windrush through the eyes of a child

Vince Reid was the youngest person on the Windrush. He came to England aged 13. From humble beginnings he rose to become a college lecturer. How did a 13 year old end up on the Windrush? According to Reid, his step-parents had three choices:

> 'They could abandon me, put me into an orphanage or take me with them. They decided to take me. I thought conditions on the boat were pretty awful, people had to entertain themselves. This took the form of boxing and some singing. Once off the boat I was so shocked at the size of the place, particularly Victoria station. However, I also remember how drab it was and because of the post-war conditions, the people looked miserable compared to Jamaica.'

What happened to you in terms of your education?

> 'I went to elementary school in Jamaica and then a Secondary Modern in Kings Cross. I was the only black child in the school. I experienced racism from the children and the staff. I began to bunk off school and it was when nobody bothered to chase me up, that I realised no one cared.'

For Vince, this negative school experience was also reflected in his poor living conditions at home.

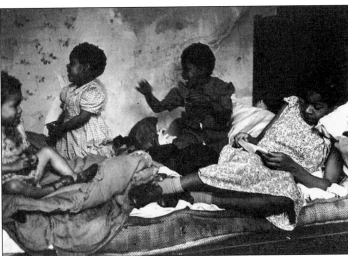

left: Vince Reid today. He was the youngest person on the Windrush aged 13.

above: Children of the Windrush.

'My father was a labourer and my mother was a dress maker. We lived in one room in Kings Cross – all three of us. It was really difficult. Too much of life was spent trying to get out of this situation.'

Eventually he joined the Air Force and after travelling the world he brought himself out of the services in 1957. This was a political decision because he was now focused on the anti-colonial battle which was now popular with countries in Africa and the Caribbean wanting independence. Vince Reid could not reconcile belonging to a force that could be used to oppress his own people. This political education continued as he joined Sussex University in 1970 as a mature student. Here, he read African History and eventually became an established teacher in a college in Brixton. Looking back, Vince does acknowledge the significant contribution that black communities have made to the life of Britain since 1948:

'We have contributed a great deal to this place. We have developed a new religion from Jamaica called Rastafari, which also gave us reggae music. We have made a great contribution to the arts and, of course, to literature and, of course, we have made this place more 'humane' with our struggle for social justice. My son and daughter have studied to University level and are aware of black history and the struggles of black people. The future lies in a wider contact of black people, particularly with those in Europe. There is a need to establish links with black communities in France and the rest of Europe to share our common experiences.'

In their small bedroom in the Clapham Shelter kenneth Murray, Eric Dryndale and Aston Robinson, three men from Kingston, Jamaica, get ready to explore London.

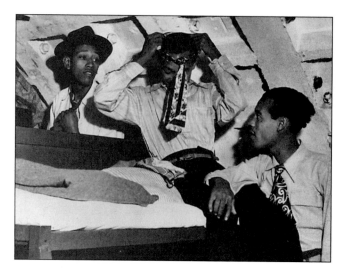

## Not a Heroes Welcome!

By the time the Windrush set off for England Baron Baker had been demobbed from the RAF. He was active in voluntary work within his community and was called upon to help make arrangements for the newcomers. He explains:

> 'At the time I was the only link between our people and the Colonial Office. I was told about the 'Windrush' by Major John Keith and so I went to see him. I asked him what preparations the Colonial Office was going to make for those people and he said none. So I suggested he use the Clapham Common Deep Shelter. They had used the Air Raid Shelter to house Italian and German prisoners of war and even myself, when I came to London some times and couldn't get a bed, I had to use it. So why not open it for the people on the 'Windrush?'

He went on:

> 'We had a long discussion about the Deep Air Raid Shelter, and finally I told Major Keith (on 22nd June 1948) that I was going on board the 'Windrush' that night and if a telegram wasn't sent to me to say the shelter was open, then I would tell the passengers on the ship that not one person should disembark until I got that assurance. I went onto the ship late that night, and about half an hour afterwards I received the telegram. So it was not until the last moment that a decision was made to open the Shelter.'

According to Alford Gardner accommodation was difficult to come by. Landladies fretted about what the the neighbours might say if they took in

above left: A Windrush arrivant neatly folds his clothes. Jamaicans kept up impeccable standards under Spartan conditions.

above right: Clapham Common, south London became a campsite as these men wait for news about work.

right: Meals at the Shelter in Clapham. English food would be another bland experience.

'coloured' lodgers and so refused to put them up. Alford Gardner and his four friends decided to buy their own house in Leeds. They had to pay-up front because banks refused to grant them reasonable mortgages. They suffered some bitter experiences when trying to get better jobs. Gardner says:

'I remember phoning-up for a job at an engineering company and being given an appointment. When I arrived and saw the secretary she told me that the job had gone. I said 'Rubbish, I spoke to the manager yesterday afternoon'. I insisted she get the manager. When he saw me he said, sorry the vacancy had gone. In those days there was nothing we could do but try somewhere else.'

Gardner also remembers the practice of wealthy landlords, both black and white, buying cheap property and renting them to the new arrivants from the

Rennick Tobis from Jamaica at the hostel set up for immigrants in Clapham air raid shelter south London.

## IMMIGRATION IN THE 1940s AND '50s

After the 492 passengers on the Empire Windrush, October 1948 saw the Orbita bringing 180 West Indians to Liverpool, and in January 1940 39 Jamaicans arrived in the city aboard the Reina del Pacifico.
The West Indian immigration figures during the 1950s looked like this:

**1950 — a few hundred**
**1951 — approximately 1,000**
**1952 — approximately 2,000**
**1953 — approximately 2,000**
1954 — 24,000
1956 — 26,000
1957 — 22,000
1958 — 16,000

By 1955 there were approximately 18,000 West Indians in London of which 3,500 lived in Lambeth, (the vast majority of whom were Jamaicans). Brixton, with well over 1,000 West Indians, was London's main area of West Indian settlement and it was Geneva and Somerleyton Roads which were at the heart of this settlement.
In 1958, ten years after the Empire Windrush, about 125,000 West Indians had come to Britain as part of the post-war immigration trend. All of these new settlers were British citizens.

Caribbean. This he regarded as exploitation, especially when the landlord would rent seven men one room. In these cases men would sleep in the same bed but in shifts. Those working at nights would swap with the day workers.

In 1963 a study of black immigrants in Notting Hill carried out by Pearl Jephcott showed that nearly three-fifths of households had the sole use of one room only. In order to survive these taxing conditions Caribbean people had to learn to work together and be resourceful. One inventive scheme was the 'Pardner' system. This was a savings system where people would pool their money each week, thus allowing one person or a group to get a substantial draw on a regular basis. Money was used for house purchase and furniture. Most people wanted to escape the trap of having their families living in single rooms. Many of the unmarried men on the Windrush would pool together with friends and buy a house as a group venture. Although many of those on the Windrush married white women, there was a tendency to 'stick together'. This was not only because of common cultural patterns but also because the host community was so unfriendly and in some cases hostile. People also settled according to their Caribbean backgrounds. Hiro (1992) writes:

> A close examination of West Indian settlements proved the seminal importance of these considerations. Since the contingent from the SS Empire Windrush was Jamaican, their place of settlement, Brixton, attracted their relatives and friends from Jamaica. The result was that 80 per cent of the West Indians in Brixton were Jamaicans. In Notting Hill and Paddington, on the other hand, the majority of the West Indians were from the smaller islands. Hiro (1992: p30)

## The making of the Promised Land

For the Windrush generation the making of the Promised Land, has a number of meanings. It can be seen as the rewards of a long journey of hope – many have seen this fulfilled in owning their own homes or seeing their children go off to University. In another sense, there was a building of a promised land in the context of 'modern Britain' – the Caribbean migrant was a vital component in the reconstruction of England after the war. The third meaning is the ability to return 'home' to the Caribbean, maybe to enjoy a healthy retirement in the sun. It is through these interpretations of the 'Promised Land' that we get an understanding of the different outcomes for this generation.

A bus driver from Birmingham begins to feel the changing mood of white people as the honeymoon turns to hostility

The work of Baron Baker exposed how inadequate the British government had been about making preparations for these new arrivants. This was a really badly planned operation and Caribbean people were really left to work out their own salvation. Soon the authorities were shamed into some sort of action but before this most were left to use their own resources and contacts in a country that needed their labour but resented their presence. The Ministry of Labour expressed its relief that the new workers had finally dispersed to different parts of the country where 'even though they did not get immediate employment, they would cease to be a recognisable as a problem.'

When he was demobbed, Baron Baker went to work as a welder. But after a while he grew bored with this, and became a chef at Earls Court Arena. The decision to open the Deep Shelter to the 'Windrush' passengers played a great part in making Brixton (within a mile of the Deep Shelter) the multi-racial community it is today, as occupants of the shelter eventually moved to lodgings in that area. Baron was asked how he felt about contributing to the making of modern Brixton:

> 'It's a very nice feeling, because when I first came you could travel over London and there were no black people to be seen. To find another black man I had to go to Aldgate East. But today every corner I go I can see four or five black people. It makes me feel proud and it makes me feel that what I've done in the past, and am doing now, has not been a waste of time.'

But the progress made over the years was slow, and Baron recalls that 'it was only by the late 1950s that you began to see black people with their own homes and cars.'

## The Notting Hill riots 1958

There are many stories that claim to explain the beginnings of the Notting Hill riots. However, there is no doubt that the events in West London and St Ann's in Nottingham was a tragic mark in British history. Put simply, black people faced the threat of being lynched in their homes and on the street as wild mobs of white youths went on the rampage. The only thing to compare to this kind of savagery was in the southern states of America. According to Pilkington (1988):

> It all began with a young Swedish woman, Majubritt Morrison who lived with her West Indian husband, Raymond…Walking down the street…One teenager pointed at her: 'There's another one, another black man's trollop!' Suddenly the crowd turned towards her, shouting 'White trash!' 'Nigger lover' 'Get her! Kill her!'  Pilkington (1988)

White demonstrations in Notting Hill, London. This was the third night in a row that whites sought to attack black people.

top: A white racist demonstrator is restrained by police.

below: Stop and search. A black man is searched after another night of fighting between black and white on the streets of Notting Hill, London.

She was hit to the ground by an iron bar and the crowd then turned on a nearby black party, Pilkington continues:

> By this time the house was full of revellers and a sound system was playing with Count Suckle – one of the first black sounds men in London – acting as disc jockey. King Dick remembers that a calypso record called *'Oriental Ball'* was playing when he heard a buzzing noise, like a swarm of bees. He went outside and there, coming towards him, was the crowd. He watched stunned, as hundreds of people approached. Then suddenly bricks and iron bars started smashing through the windows, the white crowd chanting 'Kill the niggers!' 'Keep Britain White!'

That was the start of four consecutive days and nights of race riots in Notting Hill, some of the worst outbreaks of civil unrest and racial violence in Britain this century. Black people were chased down streets, had their houses fire bombed and many were hospitalised.

In 1958 as an active member of London's Caribbean community, Baron Baker met the Jamaican Chief Minister Norman Manley, who was visiting London on a peace mission after the Notting Hill riots. While showing him around Notting Hill a policeman approached them and ordered Mr Manley to move on. Baron, never one to be slow in responding, rounded on the policeman, 'Do you know who this man is? He's my Chief Minister. If your Prime Minister visited Jamaica he wouldn't be told to move on. Show some respect.'

According to Fryer, the racial violence in Nottingham and Notting Hill was whipped up by media sensationalism as much as the ignorance of white people:

> For 18 months there had been a series of attacks on individual black people in Nottingham streets, and such attacks were becoming more frequent. On August 23, there was fighting for 90 minutes. Police claimed that this was 'a reprisal by coloured people for previous incidents recently when some of their number were attacked by white men.' Fryer (1984)

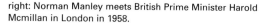

above: Chief Minister of Jamaica, Norman Manley. In London surrounded by black and white residents of Notting Hill during the race riots of 1958, as he sought to find a solution to the problems faced by the increasing number of Caribbean arrivants, settling in London.

right: Norman Manley meets British Prime Minister Harold Mcmillan in London in 1958.

However, within a day there were second and third accounts by 35 reporters who completely got the stories wrong. This led to would-be anti-black rioters the following weekend.

In the case of Notting Hill Gate a minor incident led to an eruption of fighting between black and white. The area was tense after a number of racist attacks. This flare-up made national radio and newspaper headlines, and had an immediate effect on the Notting Hill area of London, where trouble had been brewing for several weeks. Some right-wing organisations, with headquarters in the district, had been active, distributing leaflets, scrawling slogans, holding indoor meetings – generally inciting the white people to 'Keep Britain White.' Soon widespread violence broke out. At least five black people were left unconscious on the street. Black people had to quickly organise themselves and provide escort services for workers on London Transport.

The events of the summer of 1958 were viewed with much alarm by the authorities in the Caribbean. Norman Manley, the Chief Minister of Jamaica, had flown to London with the specific objective of reassuring the Caribbean migrants by touring the areas of racial disturbances and by meeting them informally. This dramatically brought to the consciousness of Britain and the world the fact that a tense racial situation was developing in the country. Writing for the New Statesman at the time of his visit Manley said:

Migration is, of course, one of the facts of life. It is as old as humanity. It is still a matter of high economic and human significance.

In modern times the white man has migrated into every coloured country that offered opportunity. But the current migration of moderately large numbers of coloured people into a white country is something new. And since race prejudice is another of the facts of life, and at its most intense where the racial difference is sharply visible – in other words, where colour is involved – the combination of race and colour prejudice is a matter with grave and serious implications

He went on:

The migration to England began when the last war was over and thousands of West Indians who had been in the armed services remained to take up life in England on the basis of the skills they had acquired during the war. It was natural that their presence here should result in a trickle of people across the seas – relatives and friends – and the trickle grew to a flood when England needed more workers to make up for the flood of her own people migrating out to Australia, Canada and all over the world

...Active violence and disorder must be stamped out swiftly and decisively. It must never be allowed to succeed. Far too much of it has succeeded in terrorising the small minority of migrants all over London and destroying their property. Manley (1958)

Claudia Jones, founder of The West Indian Gazette.

## COLOURED FOLK GET A COLD WELCOME

HUNDREDS of West Indian immigrants to this country had a cold and unfriendly welcome as they arrived at Waterloo Station on Sunday evening.

Dressed in their cotton frocks and light suits, they left the station to be greeted by about 30 men carrying "Keep Britain White" banners.

Police tried to move the demonstrators on, as the new immigrants stood in Waterloo-rd. watching quietly, showing no emotion.

Altogether 750 immigrants arrived on Sunday.

### No home

Yesterday some of the immigrants had already found their way to Brixton police station.

Some stopped to ask if the police knew of anywhere they could stay.

One couple told the station sergeant that they had some relatives "somewhere in London, and please could you help us find them."

The police told them they would have to make their own inquiries.

Providing a mouthpiece for a number of new self-help associations that grew up after the riots was the *West Indian Gazette,* a London based black monthly paper founded in March 1958 which by the end of the decade had a circulation of 15,000. Its editor, Trinidadian Claudia Jones, who had spent twenty years working with the American civil rights movement before being labelled a communist and deported, led the first black delegation to the Home Secretary after the riots. Along with Norman Manley, she opened a fund to help pay the fines of black people arrested during the disturbances. Jones had a very firm idea of the philosophy of the newspaper. It stood, she said, for the unity of West Indians and all other black people in Britain. Four months after the riots she organised, as a gesture of black solidarity and inter-racial friendship, the first Caribbean carnival in London, forerunner of the Notting Hill carnival.

The riots had a profound influence on how West Indians saw themselves, this was to continue with future generations. Their British identity had been jolted by the riots, for how could they call themselves British after being treated like unwanted strangers? This left a vacuum to be filled. 'Before the riots I was British – I was born under the Union Jack,' says Baron Baker. 'But the race riots made me realise who I am and what I am. They turned me into a staunch Jamaican. To think any other way would not have been kidding anyone else more than myself.'

Exodus for many people on the Windrush would be perceived as another homecoming. In terms of their colonial background and education Britain was the centre and they were the margins. However, Jamaican poet Louise Bennett saw this migration as doing the complete opposite. In her satirical poem, 'Colonisation in Reverse', written in response to the waves of Caribbean migration to Britain she celebrates the transforming power of Jamaican culture as it plants itself at the needy shores of its colonial master. This will not be an invasion by rape, looting and slavery but by history being turned upside down – those in the margins are now moving to the centre. The power relationships have changed – the cultural 'bag an baggage' of the migrants had to be accommodated within the reluctant host society.

*What a joyful news, Miss Mattie:*
*Ah feel like me heart gwine burs-*
*Jamaica people colonizin*
*England in reverse*

*By de hundred, by de tousan,*
*From country an town,*
*By de ship-load, by de plane-load*
*Jamaica is Englan boun.*

*Dem a pour out a Jamaica;*
*Everybody future plan*
*Is fi get a big time job*
*An settle in de motherlan.*

*What a islan! What a people!*
*Man an woman, ole an young*
*jussa pack dem bag an baggage*
*An tun history upside dung!*
*Oonoo see how life is funny,*
*Oonoo see de turnabout?*
*Jamaica live fi box bread*
*Out a English people mout*

*For when dem catch a Englan*
*An start play dem different role*
*Some will settle down to work*
*An some will settle fi de dole*
*Jane seh de dole is not bad*
*Because dey payin she*
*Two pounds a week fi seek a job*
*Dat suit her dignity*

*Me seh Jane will never fine work*
*At de rate she dah look*
*For all day she stay pon*
*Aunt Fan couch An read love-story book.*

*What a devilment a Englan!*
*Dem face war an brave de worse;*
*But ah wonderin how dem gwine stan*
*Colonizin in reverse.*

Colonialisation in Reverses! In the late fifties the British Council did help to care for students and student nurses.

left: Yvonne Tomlinson came to Britain in the 1960s she looks to nurses like Daphne Steele as inspirational.

above: Daphne Steele still lives in Ilkley, Yorkshire where she became the first black matron.

Commenting on the poem, scholar Carolyn Cooper says:

> 'Colonisation in Reverse' continues somewhat wryly to assert that if no suitably dignified jobs are forthcoming, the role-playing, Anancy-like migrant will learn to beat the system by getting on the dole. For centuries, the English in the Caribbean have boxed the bread out of the 'natives' mouth. Now, the tables appear to be turned. But few migrants could find work to suit their dignity; they are forced to do the dirty work that the English natives, themselves, consider beneath their dignity. Cooper (1993) p176

According to Alford Gardner it was just an Annacy-like mentality that was needed to build this new promised land. Annacy is the spider god from Africa. He/she represents the skill of the tricky spider to defeat the enemy or the system. However it often took direct action to survive racism, he says:

> 'We had to thank the rough-necks from Jamaica who decided that they would not take any nonsense. We must really thank these people – they made it possible for us to survive today. The white man knew from early not to mess with us, particularly if you were a Jamaican.'

## In sickness and health: Caribbean nurses tell their story

Without Caribbean nurses who came to Britain after the war, the fledgling National Health Service would have struggled to find staff. Britain after the war was desperate for these vital services in order to drag itself out of the poverty and drabness of post-war Britain. But many black staff faced discrimination and were denied promotion. The story of black women in the

Daphne's famous sister actress Carmen Monroe

right: Daphne Steele as a young midwife.

health service is still under-researched. We do know that they did survive and in some cases succeed in a system that wanted to use them rather than appreciate their gifts and skills. This point is made by Bryan, Dadzie and Scafe:

> When Black women began arriving in Britain after the second World War to provide the newly established National Health Service with much – needed Labour, we came into a service which regarded us not as potential clients but as workers. Our role was to become the nurses, cleaners and cooks who would supply and maintain the service for others. From the very beginning, the NHS had one purpose – to replenish this country's labour supply with fit, white, male workers. Six years of war and devastation had led to a renewed popular demand for 'homes fit for heroes', and this demand could not be ignored, particularly by a Labour government keen to establish itself as the champion of the working classes. The creation of the NHS enabled the needs of capitalism to be reconciled, albeit temporarily, with the demands of the people, and the import of Black woman's labour was the convenient short-term means by which this goal would be achieved. Byran et al (1985) p89

## Daphne Steele: Britain's first Black Matron

When Daphne Steele came to the UK in 1951, there were many jobs available hospitals but no one to fill them. She was born in Guyana and her father was a pharmacist, this gave her the taste for things medical, her earliest memories recall her always wanting to be a nurse. She is the sister of one of Britain's well known actresses, Carmen Monroe who starred in the hit comedy 'Desmonds'.

Unlike, others in the Caribbean she was not escaping poverty, in fact Guyana was doing fairly well economically, she just wanted to progress with her career. She recalls:

> 'It took 14 days by boat and we landed at Plymouth. We were met by a British Council official. The first thing that struck me was that a white man took my luggage and began pushing it. No white people worked in Guyana. They had all the managerial posts and would never get their hands dirty. I couldn't get used to the terraced housing. And the women on their knees cleaning the front steps. In Guyana we had people to clean for us.'

In those days, the discipline in hospitals was almost military. The care was task-oriented and nurses' lives were ruled by ward routines: 'You all but saluted. We were the soldiers and sister was the sergeant major,' says Daphne.

The parallels did not end there. Ms Steele recalls the strict rules and regulations that were set down to keep the young nurses out of trouble.

> 'You were woken up by a loud bell in the morning and had to be back in the nurses' home by 10pm and in the bedrooms by 11pm. If you stayed out late you were put on report and you couldn't walk past sister if she was in front of you – there was no overtaking.'

She did her training in London and like many black nurses faced racism from their white colleagues and patients. This suspicion and discrimination often came in the most unexpected ways. 'One sister asked a black colleague to take a plate out of the oven and couldn't really understand why she needed an oven glove. She really believed she would be able to stand the heat,' Daphne explains.

As far as the patients were concerned Daphne used a charm offensive to disarm their racism, this worked well for her because she refused to rise to their bait. However she did admit that sometimes what they needed was a good 'cussing'. She says:

> 'I did admire the Jamaican nurses for this, they didn't stand for any nonsense. We use to have Jamaican nurses fighting our battles. If a nurse felt that somebody was bullying her – a Jamaican nurse would say point me in that person's direction, Who is it, let me go and tell her about her *******'

Daphne points to the way that nursing helped to integrate all the women from different parts of the Caribbean. This was a new experience, given the limited travel that went on between islands.

Encouraged by a friendly Irish matron, she applied and got a job as matron in 1964. She became Britain's first black matron, at St Winifred's Hospital in

Ilkley, West Yorkshire. 'I earned that job-it was not a token appointment,' she said.

Looking back, Ms Steele believes that the nurses who came here from abroad brought something different to the NHS. 'Dedication, the compassion of our culture, joy and commitment.'

Mavis Stewart came to Britain and to Queen Mary's Hospital, London, from Jamaica in 1954 after a year at nursing school. On her arrival at Southampton she was struck by how cold and grey the landscape was. She watched the smoke pouring from factory chimneys and assumed they were on fire:

'Then as I climbed on to the train, I said: 'Good afternoon everybody' – it was the way I was brought up. Needless to say there was no response. Everyone was hidden behind their newspapers.' She says. 'I came from a friendly vibrant community, so this was a bit of a shock.'

Ms Stewart says she did not think about racism. She was driven by the desire to become a nurse. 'We had learnt to think of England as the mother country so I thought I was leaving one home and going to another.'

After a while she realised that not everyone felt the same:

> 'Some patients would say: 'Take your black hands off me' or ignore you outside the hospital, but that wasn't the whole story. There were some nasty people and some who were nice. You could go into a newsagent's or a grocer's shop or get on a bus and they wouldn't take your money because you were a nurse and they appreciated you.

Looking back, Ms Stewart says the more qualified she became the harder it seemed to get the breaks.

Thelma Jones came from Grenada in 1956. She was also a trained nurse and went to Leeds hospital, she says:

> 'At the time, there was a lot of travel. There wasn't much in the way of education for us – we were brought up to believe that if you wanted to better yourself in life then go to England.'

> Once I got to the hospital I found that I was shown little respect. The sisters in particular had no respect for black nurses. The patients were just as bad. I had this woman in the middle of the night shouting, 'Police, police, this black bitch is gonna kill me! Police!' And that was in the days when we used to tie them in bed. I was hurt by comments from children. They would say, 'I want a white nurse to bathe me,' and they would call me 'Chocolate Nurse', but it was a parental thing, I put it down to the way the parents brought up their children.'

May Cambridge came to Britain from Jamaica at the tender age of eighteen. She became a nurse in East Ham, east London. She was determined not to look back as she flew out to the promised land of England. But the reality was harsh. After adopting England as her home for 37 years, she decided to pack her bags and return to the island she couldn't wait to leave. May says: 'I was lucky, I was accepted for a nursing training course from home so acquiring accommodation was no problem.' But she watched the despair and hurt register on family and friends faces as they trudged for miles in search of employment and housing – only to be rejected time and time again.

May Cambridge at 18.

'Rooms were offered at the princely sum of £2.04 with six or seven people sharing facilities. You'd have to queue in the kitchen with your pot to cook. It was no use complaining you had to be grateful that you had a roof over your head.' She recalled and added: 'The no Irish, no Blacks or no dogs was no myth.'

And she maintains white Britons regarded the immigrants with scorn and jealousy feeling black people had come into their country – taken their jobs and housing while living a life of Riley – the same thoughts she feels continue. As a nurse she remembers the abuse she got from patients: 'The patients would ask you to lift your skirt and show them your tail or ask what was it like to live in trees, they would also want to know why you didn't wash or rub your skin and wonder why the dirt didn't come off.'

A young May disembarked from the luxurious Mauritania liner at Southampton dock on a cold November day in 1951. But nothing prepared her for the grey dreary place unfolding in front of her as she made the journey to the East End hospital in London that was to be her home for five years.

Verbal and mental abuse was common she says: 'Shopkeepers would ignore you and serve the white customers first, although you had been in the shop before them.' May added 'I once asked for a piece of salmon to be told that it was too expensive for me to afford and the shopkeeper made no effort to serve me.' Introductions to men were through friends but she remembers black people always had parties every weekend. 'What else could we do to relieve the frustration.'

With hindsight she regrets leaving Jamaica. 'It was hard in the West Indies but it could never have been worse.' Although five of her brothers and sisters followed her to Britain she didn't send any money home to help with their passage, which was the practice 'I discouraged them from coming because I knew what I was feeling, but they didn't listen.' She feels little has changed, her only gain is that she made enough money to buy her house in Jamaica. As far as nursing is concerned she is equally pessimistic 'Patients in the hospital still tell black nurses to go back to their own country. The only positive point is that the younger black people now have a voice and are willing to fight back.' She ominously advises 'Black people who are coming up for retirement should start preparing at least ten years ahead and try to return to their country.'

## Creating some home comforts

One of the ways in which these new black communities began to survive socially as well as psychologically was through the re-creation of Caribbean culture in England. This connection was most closely forged through the early cricket tours by the West Indies and the fanatical support for Jamaican athletes during the 1948 Olympic Games. Alford Gardner tells the story of his efforts to follow the progress of the great Jamaican sprinter Arthur Wint, who was running in the 400 metres final in the 1948 London Olympic Games, at White City stadium:

> 'When I came back from Jamaica me and my three mates got lodgings, this was unfortunately one room, mainly because no one would rent us decent accommodation. This was temporary but we still had a hard time. I remember the 1948 Olympics in White City and all four of us had huddled around a radio, listening to the commentary. The big race involved the Jamaican runner Arthur Wint. Just at the point where the race was about to start the landlady got up and turned off the radio. For us this was the equivalent of Jamaica being in the final of the world cup. When we asked her why she turned it off – she spitefully said that she was cooling down the radio because it might overheat. Mckenley and Wint running in the final and the woman turn off the radio at a crucial time!'

He went on:

> 'I have always told my eight children about the Windrush but my kids are typically English – their mothers are English. They have never been to Jamaica or shown any cultural interest.
>
> I came in 1948 and I promised my mother I would be back in five years, this never happened apart from going back on holidays. However, I have not lost my own Jamaicaness – when I go back on vacation people are shocked when I tell them that I have lived away for the last 50 years.'

One of the reasons why Alford was able to stay in touch with his 'Jamaicaness' was that, like most of the early migrants he was able to re-create his culture in

Alford Gardner fifty years on from coming to Britain on the Windrush.

right: What a win! Arthur Wint was a great runner and Jamaicans in Britain were inspired by his Olympic victory.

# The Daily Gleaner.

LARGEST CIRCULATION ESTABLISHED 1834 Price: TWOPENCE

Vol. CXIV No. 1?? KINGSTON, JAMAICA, FRIDAY, AUGUST 6, 1948. EIGHTEEN PAGES




## Berlin: Reds Ease Financial Noose

### Sudden action frees funds as Moscow talks continue

BERLIN, August 5—(AP) —The Russians relaxed today their financial blockade of Berlin for the present. The Soviet action came on the third day after western envoys talked in the Kremlin with Stalin. It was indicated the Russians might be willing to compromise on the East-West currency war, which the Russians assigned as the reason for imposing the land blockade on the strife-torn city.

Charles Giffard, British finance officer, told a news conference that the anti-Communist city government of Berlin had reached arrangement for the release of enough funds from blocked Russian mark accounts to meet its week-end payments.

A similar arrangement was reached for western sector firms, which have been in the position of not being able to meet salaries and other debts because of the Russian squeeze on money.

#### No 'Strength'

Giffard said that as far as he knew "no strings are attached" to the Russian release of funds. The city government immediately drew 25,000,000 Russian-sponsored eastern "marks" from its 350,000,000-mark fund. The British expert said he understood the withdrawals could be made at "limited rates" under the agreement.

Giffard said the "present arrangement appears satisfactory to the Western Allies." Asked why the Russians should suddenly swerve from their apparent aim of achieving financial monopoly in Berlin, he replied, "They apparently did not want to bring things to a head in Berlin while negotiations are going on elsewhere (in Moscow). The Russians appear to have agreed to the arrangement in order to permit the life of Berlin to go on for the time being."

While the land blockade remains there is no slackening of the air lift by British and North Americans. The Royal Air Force made a new record, making 308 flights with an estimated 1,500 tons of food and fuel. The United States Air Force also carried a record haul bringing 2,043 tons of supplies in 311 flights during a 24-hour period ending 2.00 p.m.

#### Talks In Moscow

MOSCOW, Aug. 5 (AP)— A new approach by the Western Powers—probably in the form of a request for a new meeting with Stalin—may be made soon, a qualified source said today. United States, British and French envoys negotiating with the Russians on the German situation received the first reactions from their capitals to Monday night's talks with Stalin. The reactions are secret.

A high authority said the reactions were reviewed last night at a Three-Power meeting here.

(Continued on page 3)

## Reds Put Up More Road Blocks

### Against British

BERLIN, Aug. 5 (AP)—Border police said today the Russians were putting up more road blocks on the British-Soviet zone border near Lueneberg.

A dispatch from Hamburg reporting this development said small roads crossing the border in the area were being closed. Russians were digging ditches through roads and felling trees across them.

Russians said 43 trains would be made available for exhibitors and buyers from Western Germany at the Leipzig fair in their zone late this month.

A United States transport official predicted that no train would be permitted to leave the North American zone for the fair unless the Berlin blockade was lifted.

Train traffic to and from the Russian zone was cut off last month in retaliation for the Berlin blockade.

## U.S. Demands Full Share For West In Danube Control

BELGRADE, Aug., 5: (AP)—The United States today demanded full share for Western Powers in control of Danube River shipping, accusing Russia of trying to impose a monopoly by the Communist states of eastern Europe.

United States Ambassador Cavendish Cannon placed before the Danubian conference a United States plan for the river. But first he denounced the Russian proposal introduced previously as giving Russia and all her neighbours "special privileges" in Europe's most important waterway.

The United States plan would provide for a Danubian commission of eleven nations: Austria, Bulgaria, Czechoslovakia, Hungary, Rumania, the Ukraine, Russia, Yugoslavia, France, the United States, Britain.

Under the Soviet plan, membership would be limited to Danube countries, excluding Austria, until a peace treaty was signed. The United States proposal would give Germany a seat when that country gets a peace treaty "or before that time" if agreement can be reached by other members of the commission.

### Miami Air Tragedy

MIAMI, FLORIDA, August 5: (Reuter)—Six people were killed here late today when a Navy Dakota collided with a small private training plane.

The two men in the training plane baled out and were unhurt.

### Royal Holiday

LONDON, August 5: (Radio)—The King and Queen with Princess Elizabeth and Princess Margaret have left London for their Summer holiday at Balmoral. The Duke of Edinburgh will travel to Balmoral later.

Queen Mary has gone to Sandringham where she will be staying for some time.

### OFF THE RECORD

"Strebor" commenting on Sun Canter, "the colt in the Anticipation Stakes did the slow time of 1.5," when he really gets going he ought to do the distance in nothing flat.

• • •

Moscow is silent, Allied capitals hum, and Berliners whistle.

• • •

Advt. "£0000000 Gold Rush" . . . more rush than gold evidently.

• • •

Headline "Farmers ought to grasp the helping hand of Government". Some farmers think it ought to read "help the grasping hand of Government."

• • •

In a letter to the "Gleaner" Mr. B. Facey writes "when the traffic moves down King Street pedestrians cross from North to South." . . . Quite a long crossing!

• • •

The Argentine fencers in the Olympics seem very "touche".

• • •

Olympic womens' broad jumped—J. M. V. D. Kade-Koudijs, Holland . . . Another olympic record, initials

'Black Streak Of Velvet'

A remarkable photograph of Arthur Wint in action.

## Jamaica did it ... and 'God Save The King' was played for the first time

# WINT FIRST IN 400-METRE FINAL

## Equals Olympic 46.2 Record

## McKENLEY 2nd

(Special cable to the "Gleaner" from our London correspondent) (Gleaner copyright, 1948)

LONDON, August 5.—"God Save The King" was heard for the first time in the Olympic Victory Ceremony at Wembley today—but it was Jamaica that did it, as giant-striding Arthur Wint triumphed in the 400 metre final in 46.2 seconds over his highly fancied team-mate, Herbert McKenley.

We had repeatedly heard the winners feted with the "Star Spangled Banner," the Swedish, Dutch, Austrian; Tukish, every country's anthem, it seemed, except Britain's national hymn.

To-day, little Jamaica came to the rescue, and it was a moving moment when, having no National Anthem of her own, she was content for the R.A.F. band, at last, to strike up "God Save the King", in honour of her victors on the Olympic rostrum.

#### 60.000 Roar

I had never hoped to see a finer 400-metre race than this final in which Wint, to the roars of a crowd of 60,000 beat his fellow-Jamaican by a yard, and equalled the Olympic record of 46.2 secs.

There was a hush in the Stadium as the two Jamaicans, three Americans (Whitfield, Bolen and Guida), and the Australian, Curotta, came out into the arena, jogged about to loosen their muscles and relieve their tense nerves and then crossed the grass to set their starting traps.

Rain had stopped, and now the sun gleamed through a damp haze hanging over the Stadium.

The two Jamaicans were luckily drawn in next door lanes—numbers 2 and 3—with Whitfield, the chief danger, in number 4.

As the runners stripped off their track suits and crouched in their starting traps, absolute stillness came over the Stadium. The stillness was cut by the starters "Set"—and then the pistol-crack for a perfect start.

#### McKenley Sets Pace

McKenley, as expected, made the running. He had planned to cover the first 200 metres in 21 secs., and run the others off their feet, and but for Wint, he would have succeeded.

McKenley went up on the runners in the outside lanes with incredible speed and even Wint, striding out magnificently, was a full yard behind as the two Jamaicans turned into the back straight.

Coming round inside Wint, McKenley gained at least another yard, and when the runners went into the long home-stretch, only the two Jamaicans were in it.

In their white vests and dark red shorts, they were right out in front; and then began a tremendous battle to the tape. McKenley's stride shortened a little, and Wint seemed to plunge forward and gave the impression of bounding up the straight like a huge dog.

Gaining a fraction on his fellow countryman at every stride, Wint caught and passed McKenley fifteen yards from the tape to win a perfectly judged race by a yard.

McKenley's time was 46.4 secs. and he easily held off a late challenge from Whitfield, who finished two yards behind in third place.

Wint's triumph, and McKenley's second, were very popular with the crowd—now a little satiated with American victories—and Wint is regarded with spe-

(Continued on page 16)

## Jamaica's Proudest Moment

### Wint: 'I did not know I had it in me'

LONDON, Aug. 5 (Reuter)—Giant striding Arthur S. Wint of Jamaica who today equalled the Olympic record of 46.2 seconds to win the men's 400 Metres Final, did not expect to win.

He said after the race: "Frankly I did not expect to catch Herb McKenley (this fellow Jamaican whom he beat into second place). I gave it everything I had because we wanted it between us and I did not want any one breaking in on us. I did not know I had it in me."

Wint and McKenley went back to the dressing room together surrounded by a group of admiring, delighted supporters from Jamaica.

"I can tell you this is Jamaica's proudest moment," J. R. Bunting, Jamaican team manager said as he screened his runners from swarming autograph hunters.

Herbert Macdonald, overseas personnel manager for the Jamaican team said: "The great moment has come. I always felt we would do it."

## Red Malayan Rebels Battle British Force

SINGAPORE, Aug. 5 (AP)—Malayan Communist insurgents met British forces in open battle, 80 miles south of the Siamese border.

A British Army communique yesterday said British forces under cover of rocket-firing Spitfires are driving forward against stiff enemy opposition.

First reports did not indicate the scope of the battle. Presumably it was on a small scale. It is believed, however, to be the first time the Communists have stood and fought since the revolt began in June. It was the first time reports from the forward area have used the word battle.

The communique said entrenched Communists opened fire with machineguns and rifles upon a British column which was striking toward Pula in South Kelantan state, which is a Communist stronghold.

The column was held up by the fire and radioed for RAF help. A later report said the British column—a joint military and police force—has resumed its advance.

At least one Gurkha soldier was reported killed.

### Wants Wallace For Questioning

WASHINGTON, Aug. 5—(AP) Representatibe Rankin, Democrat of Mississippi, issued a statement today proposing that House investigators call Henry Wallace, the Progressive Party presidential candidate, for questioning about the "placing of Communists" in "key positions" in the Commerce Department.

Rankin said the House Un-American Activities Committee, of which he is a member, has received testimony that a large number of individuals "charged with being Communist spies worked in the Department during the time Wallace was Secretary of Commerce under Roosevelt.

## Kirkwood Notes U.S. 'Interference'

### Tells Of Obstacles In Getting Citrus Contracts

A veiled attack on the United States of America for "interfering" in the "family affairs" of the British Commonwealth of Nations, was made by the Hon. R. L. M. Kirkwood, Member of the Legislative Council, speaking yesterday at a meeting of the Citrus Growers Association, Limited, of which he is president.

Telling of his efforts in England to obtain contracts for the CGA to supply citrus fruit and juice to Great Britain on a long-term basis, Mr. Kirkwood, who is also the Jamaican agent of the West Indies Sugar Company, subsidiary of the giant British Tate and Lyle organisation, said,

"There are, I think, certain obstacles in the way. Shall I say that these obstacles are of an international nature? Shall I say that in matters of this description, whatever the goodwill towards Jamaica and other parts of the British Commonwealth that exists—and I think it does exist on the part of His Majesty's Government—there are other countries, or especially another country, which appears to have a great say in our future destinies; to have a great interest in the internal arrangements which have been concluded or might be concluded between members of the British Commonwealth of Nations?

#### The Future

"Whether that say, that influence, is a desirable thing I am not prepared to descant on at the present time. You members of this association will probably draw your own

(Continued on page 3)

### Ford Prices Up

DETROIT, Aug. 5.— (AP)—Ford Motor company has announced price increases averaging five per cent on all new Ford cars except one model. They amount to 75 dollars on each car.

At the same time the company reduced the price of its six cylinder business coup by five dollars.

Ford said it was forced to raise prices for the second time in less than two months because of higher material and labour cost; and the "necessity for reducing present production volume due to material shortage which caused production interruptions."

## BRITISH PLAN ARMS SHIFT PROBE

LONDON, Aug. 5 (AP)—Britain has ordered an investigation of the transfer of certain Army equipment to Egypt from British stores at Rafa on the Palestine-Egyptian frontier, the foreign office announced.

Israel has complained to the United Nations that such a transfer took place July 29 and constituted a breach of the Palestine truce.

The Foreign Office spokesman said an "ordinary commercial transaction involving certain Army stores" took place and details are awaited on the nature of equipment sold to the Egyptians. He said so far as he knew the equipment was of non-military character.

Foreign Minister Moshe Shertok, of Israel, has told the United Nations the material included "military equipment, especially electrical instruments, searchlights and the like."

He said the equipment later was forwarded to Egyptian-held villages in the Negeb desert area of Southern Palestine, about 25 miles from Tel Aviv.

### Jews Make Bid For Peace Parley

TEL AVIV, Aug. 5 (AP)—Israel's Government today asked Count Folke Bernadotte to transmit its invitation to Arab nations for peace talks. Count Bernadotte is the United Nations Mediator for Palestine.

It was the first move by the new Jewish state to arrange a peace treaty conference. Foreign Minister Moshe Shertok talked with the Mediator three hours and then told him. "I approach you as Mediator officially on behalf of the Provisional Government of Israel, to transmit to the belligerent powers an invitation to meet the Provisional Government for peace negotiations."

### St. Mary Water Supplies Discussed

A deputation from the St. Mary Parochial Board yesterday forenoon waited on Mr. J. S. Mordecai, Assistant Secretary at the Secretariat, and Mr. Richardson of the same Department, and discussed with them matters pertaining to water supplies.

The deputation was led by Mr. C. L. Clemetson, Chairman of the Board, other members were Mr. N. L. Marsh, vice Chairman, Mr. C. L. A. Stewart, Mr. R. Thompson, Mr. B. H. Philpotts, Clerk of the Board and Mr. R. Spicer, Superintendent of Roads and Works of the parish.

The deputation first dealt with the White River water supplies scheme as it affects St. Mary, and also the filtration of the High Gate and Richmond water supplies.

### Shell Blasts Rock Jerusalem

JERUSALEM, August 5. A series of shell explosions rocked Jerusalem today following a night of gunfire. A Press statement issued by the Israeli Ministries for Foreign Affairs and Defence said the Trans-Jordanian Arab Legion and the Egyptian Army, facing the Jewish area from points in northern, eastern and southern Jerusalem, directed automatic weapon and mortar fire at various forward Jewish positions. No casualties or damage were reported.

In Israeli communique said five Arabs were hit when Jewish troops returned fire.

### Shot Dead By Ranger

GOLDEN GROVE, August 5 (From Our Correspondent) George Powell a former labourer employed to Jamaica Sugar Estates, who was shot by a ranger on Holland Estate, was found dead in a canefield with two bunches of bananas beside him

## 'Open Order' For Japanese Cotton Goods

All types of cotton textiles made in Japan, printed or processed in that country, can be imported into Jamaica and the trade is being invited to submit applications for these licences.

Importers can apply for "any quantity they may desire", according to Mr. G. C. Gunter, Trade Controller.

These transactions are to be on a 100 per cent sterling basis. Items ordered from or through Boekicho (Board of Trade) may be delivered to colonial traders' representatives in Jamaica for processing and subsequent export to the colony, payment [illegible]

Opening up of this market in such extensive form is calculated to provide a big supply of economy textiles for Jamaica, without expenditure of valuable dollars.

### All's Well At The Dam

Hermitage Dam is holding out nicely, according to readings yesterday. There is a storage of 407½ million gallons, with an inflow of 5,400,000 from Wag and Moresham rivers. Consumption was 5,340,000 gallons.

Meanwhile the Water Commission has been pushing its projects for new supplies which should be ready in good time.

## And The Farmers Cheered

A cheer went up during a meeting of the Citrus Growers Association in Ramson Hall, Kingston yesterday forenoon when it was announced that Wint and McKenley had run first and second in the 400 metres at the Olympics.

Said the Hon. R. L. M. Kirkwood, chairman of the association, making the announcement: "Gentlemen, an important piece of news has just been whispered to me by Mr. C. L. A. Stuart, which I am sure any Jamaican meeting can be interrupted to announce"

"Wint and McKenley have come first and second in the 400 metres."

#### Cable Sent

When the spontaneous cheer that rose from the hall died down, Mr. Kirkwood added: "I propose that we send them a cable from this meeting, congratulating them on their splendid effort and wonderful achievement for Jamaica. We are all proud of them."

Mr. Kirkwood raised a laugh from his audience when he quipped finally: "We will ask

(Continued on page 14)

## Derby Sweepstake Figures

The following statement on the August Sweepstake, to be drawn on the Jamaica Derby at Knutsford Park to-morrow, was issued yesterday by Knutsford Park Ltd.:—

The Directors,
Knutsford Park Limited,
KINGSTON.

Gentlemen:—

We have audited the Books, Vouchers and Records of the Jamaica-British West Indies Sweepstake based on the Jamaica Derby, legally conducted by Knutsford Park Ltd., under authority of Chapter 425 of the Revised Statutes of Jamaica, which Sweepstake will be drawn publicly at Knutsford Park Race Course on 7th, August, 1948.

Counterfoil No. E. X. 10751 for which cash has been received, and Official Seller's Receipt No. 18077 dated 16th, July, 1948 issued, has not been presented for audit, and consequently will not be included in the draw.

We certify that in our opinion the undermentioned figures are correct according to the information and explanations given to us and as shown by the Books and Vouchers of the Sweepstake.

| | | |
|---|---|---|
| Number of Tickets entered in the draw: 158,839 at 4/- each | | £31,767 14 0 |
| Less 24,385 Bonus Tickets issued to Vendors | £4,877 0 0 | |
| Cash Commission paid to Vendors | 1,041 5 6 | 5,918 5 6 |
| | | £26,049 10 6 |

Under the Law and in accordance with the Terms published on the back of each Ticket sold, the sum of £26,049 10. 6 is distributable as follows:—

| | | |
|---|---|---|
| Government Stamp Duty | | £1,331 19 10 |
| Jamaica Hospitals | | 3,907 8 7 |
| Promoters | | 4,341 11 9 |
| Purses | | 1,000 0 0 |
| Expenses | | 4,702 5 8 |
| PRIZES: | | |
| 2 Drawers of Winning Horse | £2,000 each | 4,000 0 0 |
| 2 " " Second | £500 " | 1,000 0 0 |
| 2 " " Third | £250 " | 500 0 0 |
| 2 " " Fourth | £125 " | 250 0 0 |
| 500 Cash Prizes | £4 18 4 each | 2,450 4 8 |
| 42 Drawers of other Horses | £40 9 6 " | 1,700 0 0 |
| 2 Sellers of 2 Winning Tickets | £106 5 0 " | 212 10 0 |
| 2 " " 2 Second | £53 2 6 " | 106 5 0 |
| 2 " " 2 Third | £31 17 6 " | 63 15 0 |
| 2 " " 2 Fourth | £21 5 0 " | £42 10 0 |
| 42 " " other Tickets drawing Horses | £10 2 4 " | £425 0 0 |
| | | £26,049 10 6 |

Yours faithfully,
(Sgd.) H. C. NUNES
Chartered Accountant
(Sgd.) G. W. N. DOWNER
Chartered Accountant

Kingston Jamaica, B.W.I.
5th August, 1948.

SCHEDULE OF EXPENSES

Printing and Stationery £1,004 15 7, Rent £130, Salaries and Wages £2,318 17 10, Advertising £483 9 5, Postages and Telegrams £340 9 1, Audit Fees £315, General Operating Expenses £136 13 .6. Total £4,702.-5. 8

## Arias, Again In Exile, Says Life Is Endangered

BALBOA, C.Z., Aug. 5: (AP)—Declaring "My life is in danger," Arnulfo Arias Madrid former President of Panama, fled into political exile Wednesday for the second time."

Arias, who was the opposition candidate for President in the elections last May, declared as he boarded a plane for Barranquilla, Colombia.

"We are under a dictatorial regime. A horrid criminal fraud has been perpetrated. I will return when a sense of responsibility and tranquility return to Panama."

His reference to "fraud" apparently was aimed at the outcome of the May presidential race. He claimed victory in the unofficial count but the official tally, announced after months of counting gave a slight edge to his government-backed opponent, Domingo Diaz Arosemena.

Arias spent four years away from Panama, in exile after being ousted from the presidency in 1941. His flight into the United States-controlled Canal Zone was his second in a month. He fled Panama on July 4 after a shooting affray involving members of his party and police. He went back July 19

## Typhoid Outbreak In St. Thomas

A typhoid outbreak has hit the parish of St. Thomas and threatens to spread unless immediate measures are taken. Since Monday, three cases have been discovered by the MOH, Dr. A. A. Bonner,

Seat of the outbreak is the Arcadia district in eastern St. Thomas. Probe undertaken by Dr. Bonner immediately upon discovery of the first case has traced the causes to the village water supply. Yesterday at the meeting of the Parochial Board, Dr. Bonner told the Board that the water supply would have to be closed at once, or the result would be "another Port Antonio".

#### TELEGRAMS RUSHED

Hurry telegrams were immediately dispatched to the Colonial Secretariat by the Board in session, and orders given to the Parochial Superintendent to prepare signs for erection at the location of the supply last night or early today.

Meanwhile, pending Government assistance in cleaning up the system, attempts will be made by the Board to convey drinking water by a road sprinkler. But this, it is acknowledged, will not be enough.

Arcadia is a district of 500 people east of Port Morant. The supply is obtained from a spring, which runs partly underground. Where the water breaks the surface, a concrete covering is erected over it for protection. There is a hole in the centre of this covering for cleaning pur

(Continued on page 3)

### New British Guiana River Discovered

GEORGETOWN, British Guiana, Aug. 5— Strickland Ottley, former Royal Air Force flying officer, reports that he has discovered a new river in the British Guiana hinterland.

Ottley said the new stream runs across a plateau 2,000 feet above sea level in the vicinity of the Anu and Konawaruk rivers, both tributaries of the Potaro river. (From Miami Herald).

### Village Bombed, But With Flour

BERLIN, August 5. (Reuter). A United States supplies plane on the air lift to Berlin bombed a Russian zone village with sacks of flour today, jettisoning part of its load because of engine trouble. More than a ton of flour was dropped. The plane made a safe landing at Templehof airport, Berlin.

Black people made their own entertainment.

Britain. From the very earliest days of post-war black settlement, African Caribbean people began to re-build and adapt their cultural and leisure institutions to life in Britain. The need for such institutions was enhanced by the harsh realities of the racism they experienced. They built on the existing networks of jazz clubs that already existed in London.

Soon there emerged a number of black-owned clubs and drab old London was injected with life from the diaspora – there was calypso, Latin, jazz and R&B.

However it was the private leisure activities that was created within the black community that we find the most vital source of comfort. This ranged from wedding receptions, church gatherings to bank holiday outings. Hinds observes that the radiogram became 'a standard piece of furniture' in every black dwelling. The Saturday night party was a key social ritual which provided entertainment for this new and young generation. It was through these institutions that the mighty force of Jamaican music became established in Britain's new and old black communities. According to Simon Jones (1988):

> As a consequence of the 1958 {Notting Hill violence}, the early 1960s saw the emergence of a culturally more self-sufficient and cohesive Afro-Caribbean community in Britain. The 1960s as a whole 'colony society' in the larger areas of black settlement as a defensive corporate response to the more pronounced forms of public racism in British society. This winning of cultural space, in which an alternative black social life could flourish, was most noticeable in the expansion of autonomous cultural, economic and leisure institutions within black communities throughout Britain. Black restaurants, cafes, churches, food shops and a network of night-clubs and record shops emerged to cater for the cultural and recreational needs of Afro-Caribbean people. Jones (1988) p20

Sound systems began to appear in the late 1950s, they were developed into mobile music services that played at parties or dance halls. This became the cultural newspaper of life in Jamaica and helped to sustain a besieged people. Soon this would be the source in which a distinctively black British sound would be created.

## Hitting Britain for six: How cricket gave us pride

One of the purposes of Carnival was that the slaves used it as a way of defying their masters once a year – dressing-up like them and mocking them in a street parody. It gave them some power for a while in a relationship that was cruelly oppressive. In the same way the touring of a black West Indian team to Britain would give pride, relief and revenge to those excluded from mainstream society.

Caribbean people adopted cricket in the same way they changed Christian worship. They gave it their own rhythm and style. Cricket was the perfect gift to the colonised just as Christianity lent itself, from the 18th century, to Caribbean manipulation. This was seen in Caribbean forms of worship ranging from pocomania to Rastafari worship.

The audience at a West Indian cricket match is an integral part of the drama. Every ball played is commented on with wit, raucous humour and wonderful use of language which is the 'West Indian way.' So the early West Indian cricketers, even when they were losing, were brashly and defiantly beautiful to behold!

Many will confess to being totally bowled over or caught silly off guard (or mid-on) by the arrogant sensuality of the striding men in white, against dark skins advancing with stylish swagger towards the crease. The three Ws were famous for their physiques. And Gary Sobers 'walked a way' in his pads according to many ecstatic female informants.

Jimmy Carnegie, the Jamaican sportswriter, is of the view that in cricket as in several other sports the most elegant performances are also in themselves, art objects and represent 'poetry in motion' – in short dance.

Professor R. Nettleford sees it more akin to dance and he further cites Brian Lara, Carl Hooper in the field, bowling and also at bat, Jeffrey Dujon with bat and behind the wicket, Alvin Kallicharan, Lawrence Rowe, Rohan Kanhai, the great Gary Sobers, Seymour Nurse, Roy Fredericks and Conrad Hunte, and perhaps the father of them all the late Frank Worrell. He describes Bernard Julien as being like Lara in the 'Sagaboy' tradition (a well known performance tradition) of their native Trinidad and Tobago. The great 'dancer-players'

1950 – The three Ws. Frank Worrell in play in the third Test at Nottingham when he made 261. Everton Weeks and Clyde Walcott.

63

left: Big Cat! Former West indies captain Clive Lloyd inspires the West Indies to another convincing victory.

above: The end of the fifth Test of 1984 against England – Blackwash!

with the ball he feels to be Michael Holding, Sonny Ramadhin and Gary Sobers who shared that panther-like fielding style with Rohan Kanhai, Clive Lloyd, Viv Richards and Roger Harper.

James Adams and Curtley Ambrose danced that post-victory waltz shown world-wide in a Reuters photo in celebration of the 'fall of another New Zealand wicket as the home team failed to save the follow-on on the third day.' Adams and Ambrose, like all their colleagues and fore-fathers, dance their way to victory in the normal course of play. The congratulatory 'high fives' after a brilliant ball, a resulting catch or high-scoring stroke makes for a beautiful choreographic design during a game. What is ironic is that the modern day English team have copied this style. It would mark a characteristic of popular culture, that whatever black people invented it would soon be appropriated by a white population hungry to free itself from a stiff-upper lip.

For Alford Gardner the sweet victory of the West Indies in England was better than any food-parcel from home. The crowds were also part of the performance, for the first time in Britain the gentlemen's game of cricket had been taken over by the masses. Gardner tells the story of the pride and tension that greeted the post-war West Indian victories:

> 'There was a man who I use to work with. We would get the bus together. He never used to speak to me, but he broke his silence when the West Indies looked like losing their warm-up game against a University team. He told me that the students had set a one day score that was unbeatable. The next evening I met him, after one West Indian player had polished off their runs. He refused to say anything and looked so upset. He never took the same bus with me again. The West Indies made us walk tall, especially at work.'

Black congregation at worship, 1970.

right: Doing their own thing! Jamaican pastor F.S. Wallen and Mrs Wallen of the Church of God, Effra Road, Brixton, 1961.

## The Church

The real shock for most of these arrivants was just how unfriendly and in some cases racist, the English churches were. The reception was frosty, nobody said 'Hello'. English people would often sit apart from the new Caribbean visitors or would walk away from the pew in which they were sitting. In the early fifties in Wolverhampton, of the six Pentecostal churches, only one managed to retain a substantial number of Caribbean people. Reluctantly, the guests decided to build their own churches and worship God in their own way. Each Sunday these churches began to grow. It was the Pentecostal church that soon became the first Caribbean institution in Britain. The church was not just a centre for worship, it acted as structure for social activity and the preservation of Caribbean identity.

## Making new friends

In the early 1950s there were few women from the Caribbean coming to Britain. It was not until 1955, when the numbers began to even out. In the early days 85 per cent of the West Indian newcomers were men, most of whom were single. Consequently, black men used to go out with local white women and they often married.

This was the time of the infamous period of Rachmanism. Baron Baker eventually found a room of his own in West London, having spent a year relying on charity and friends. Notting Hill was the centre of the empire of the notorious landlord, Peter Rachman. His fortune was made through cunning manipulation of his tenants and the new liberal rent laws. West Indians formed a large proportion of Rachman's tenants. They could be charged extortionate rents, as they had nowhere else to live; they could be forced into multi-occupation and charged per head. By 1958 he owned around 100 houses in the

West London area. To Rachman West Indians were a friend in need of his terrible hospitality.

It was by luck that Baker came across Mrs Fisher in Tavistock Road, she was a landlady prepared to take black tenants. Baron Baker says: 'Her neighbours used to call her white-trash-nigger-lover because she associated with us, But she was liberal-minded and didn't care. Her rooms were all rented and she made plenty of money. She laughed at her neighbours because they weren't enjoying the life she was enjoying.'

Most of the friends that the new arrivants made outside their own community were white women – this was clearly a sexual attraction but, according to Horace Ove, women were the only sympathetic people who reached out to black men. He says: 'It wasn't that white women fancied this 'gigolo out of the jungle' as people used to make out. They were curious, and despite pressure from their parents and friends they helped us by reaching out to us. They had an understanding for us for some reason.'

Perhaps one of the reasons why some white women felt an empathy with black men was that they also knew what it was like to be an expendable commodity. During the war they were considered indispensable. However, when peace came they were expected to go back to the home and the kitchen. In the same way those men from the Caribbean who had served in the RAF were now expected to return to the plantation.

As more and more West Indian clubs began to open, they attracted the good, the bad and, unusually, the very rich. In this sense perhaps some white women were not just looking to comfort the poor downtrodden brothers but they wanted 'colour' and the 'exotic'. Anything to take them away from the drab and limited existence, According to Pilkington (1988):

West Indian men mixed with women of all classes and backgrounds, from the very poor to the very rich. One woman who made a regular appearance on the West Indian scene was Sarah Churchill, Winston's favourite child.

Racism in Brixton during the fifties – KBW means 'Keep Britain White.'

left: Many black men married local women during the fifties. These relationships had to endure a lot of prejudice.

right: White women according to Horace Ove were often the only people who showed any empathy. This led to many mixed relationships.

She used to hang around with us,' says Baron Baker. He met her in the Sunset Club and Calypsonian King Dick spent many evenings with her at Totobag's. She would arrive in her Rolls Royce and, leaving her driver sitting outside, mingle with the crowd until closing time in the early hours. For her, as for Colin MacInnes mixing with black men was a way out of her restrained social circle, an escape from high-society prudery. Pilkington (1988)

London's Notting Hill is now known as a real melting-pot. It is an area where the rich, poor, black and white mix happily. Black people endured so much pain both psychological and physical in order to carve their space in order to make this area multiracial. This needs to be remembered, given that racist attacks are still a phenomenon of life in Britain's big cities.

The Empire Windrush generation has produced a first and second generation of black Britons who were born in the 'mother country'. For many of those early arrivants, the exodus did not lead to a promised land but to a world of ambivalence. Many expected to remain only for a few years. However, as time passed it became increasingly difficult for them to return to a changing Caribbean. Some did make the trip back and others have waited until retirement. For the majority, there is a real sense of bitterness that their children and grandchildren are still struggling with a host country that is stubbornly hostile to black people.

Horace Ove, rejected as an interior designer when he first came to Britain in the 1950s, soon became an established film maker. He believed that the impact of the riots and of the Caribbean experience during the 1950s have profoundly influenced the attitudes of the younger generation of black people born in Britain. 'The fifties generation are bitter and they are sad. You can see that coming through their children. Young black people can see how their parents were treated and have no intention of allowing that to happen to them.'

BLAC
MOV
BRUTALIT
BLACK YOUTH
BETT
EDUCA
TOP POLI
HARRASSM
ROUND SCHO
PUBLIC
DEMAND
VIOLENCE
BLACK

# I'm Black and I'm Proud (1970–1980)

*Say it loud, I'm Black and I'm proud*

James Brown


Natty Dread taking over... Culture

*Now, I've been brought up in a society all my life where we were looked on as black people not having beauty. It was all blonde and white where real beauty was. When I got to the States, that was to have quite a psychological effect, that we are a proud and beautiful people. As I was going around America I just wanted to be around black people, 'cos I could appreciate beauty in a way I'd never met and seen before, and that was quite profound at that time. And then they were moving into Afros at that time and I saw little children with Afros, and I always used to say, when I have my own children, my little boy's going to have an Afro.*

Paul Stephenson

previous page: Black parents organised to support their children against continual arrests and alleged harrassment by the police. In North London in June 1975 the Black Parents Movement and the Black Youth Movement were formed.

# I'M BLACK AND I'M PROUD (1970–1980)

The period 1970–1981 sees the children of the Windrush as teenagers and young adults. What did Britain have in store for this generation? The period was marked by two key factors. First the continual harassment of the state and the police of black youth on the street through the police using the old vagrancy Act of 1824 commonly known as the Sus Laws. Second, and partly in response to the first was the rise of Rastafarian faith in Britain. It was a period that was significant for its desire to find 'roots' and 'ancestral links'. There was a journey into what can simply be called nationalism and authenticity. Racism had emptied any possibility of black integration into the mainstream of British life. It was marked by the slogan of the National Front: 'There Ain't No Black in the Union Jack' Therefore the Caribbean, Africa and America – symbolically represented the new Promised land to the next generation.

## Exodus

According to writer Caryl Phillips (1987):

> It was in the United States that I made the 'discovery' that it was possible for a black person to become, and sustain a career as, a writer. My ignorance probably came about as a result of my education and my own lack of a coherent sense of identity in 1970s Britain. (1987: p1)

There was a similar sense of alienation at the heart of the black British experience compared to the Windrush generation. Phillips talks about being at school and never having a text or lesson concerning black people. He goes on:

> About three years later, one of the most painful episodes of my childhood took place. This time it was inside a classroom. Mr. Thompson, an English literature teacher, decided to demonstrate his knowledge of all things by explaining the origins of our surnames. So Greenberg was Jewish, Morley originally came from the small Yorkshire town of the same name, and Mckenzie was a Scot. I felt a hot flush of embarrassment long before he turned towards my desk. 'Phillips' he mused, 'you must be from Wales.' The whole class laughed, while I stared back at him stony-faced, knowing full well I was not from Wales. The truth was I had no idea where I was from as I had been told I was born in the Caribbean but came from England. I could not participate

in the joke in which my identity was a source of humour. Even those I considered my friends were laughing. If the teaching of English literature can feed a sense of identity then I, like many of my Black contemporaries in Britain, was starving. Phillips (1987) p2

Phillips looks back on the seventies and suggests that it must have been one of the worst decades to grow up in since the Second World War. The crazy fashions of this period and years of power-cuts and strikes left the period with a bad mark. However, he does point to the roots reggae of the seventies led by Bob Marley as a light in a time of darkness.

Caryl Phillips, he needed to go to America to find confidence in being Black.

The period would be marked by a search for 'roots' and 'identity' in a first generation who was born in Britain but never felt a sense of belonging.

One of the best summaries of the plight of black youth in Britain was written by academic Chris Mullard in 1973:

We are different from our parents in many ways. The only home we know is Britain...All the statutory and voluntary white agencies have now adopted the white race experts' label – 'second generation immigrants' – for black Britons. By the use of such labelling devices the vicious circle of racial discrimination becomes institutionalised and perpetuated. Merely because of the colour of their skin, black children become second-class citizens, doomed to a life of ostracism, exploitation, difference...

We will not put up with racist behaviour. Rather than acquiesce we will react. Through our understanding of the British way of life we will be better equipped than our parents to organise constructive rebellion...

We are now heading towards a complete breakdown in communication between white and black society. This process began in the early sixties and gathered momentum...with the emergence of Powellism and the country's expressed wish to tighten up controls and ostracise (and possibly later on repatriate) black immigrants and black Britons alike. We cannot help but feel that white society is knifing us in the back...Most of us have withdrawn our co-operation from official

Bob Marley surrounded by fans on a visit to London.

agencies and have organised resistance to race relations policy and the meddling of whites in our affairs. This resistance has been passive in the tradition of civil disobedience...But as the breakdown in communication becomes more and more absolute, passive resistance could give way to more violent forms of behaviour.

This could happen in the next decade when the majority of black people living in Britain will be like me – black British...Unless steps are taken immediately, we shall be filled with more hatred and bitterness than our black American brothers. Enoch Powell has predicted race riots in this country by 1986. For completely different reasons I see violent expressions of our position in and disgust with white society some years before then. Mullard (1973)

In fact the Watershed came in 1981 in Brixton, which saw one of worst street battles between black youth and police. The seventies will always be known for having the worst relations between black youth and the police. Right through the 1970s, Britain's black communities had been under attack from Fascists and police. They had been forced to defend themselves, since nobody else could or would defend them. The rebellion of black youth in the inner cities was the logical and, as is now clear, inevitable response to racist attacks. It was the culmination of years of harassment. Its message was simply: 'We have had enough.'

The Black Power movement in America had a major influence on Britain. Here, Stockely Carmicheal addresses meeting. Michael X black activist is second left.

In 1960 there were approximately 125,000 West Indians in Britain who had arrived since the war. British industry gladly absorbed them because there was a serious shortage of labour. These new immigrants from the colonies regarded themselves as 'English'.

However, between 1958 and 1968 the honeymoon was over, with black people facing racist attacks and suffering discrimination, particularly in housing. It was the question of immigration and nationality that was the breaking-point, and it is still a key issue today. Peter Fryer (1984) points to this attack on the cultural citizenship of West Indian immigrants as the main weapon of racism against those early settlers:

> Between 1958 and 1968 black settlers in Britain watched the racist tail wag the parliamentary dog. It was a sustained triumph of expediency over principle...The problem was not white racism, but the black presence; the fewer black people there were in this country the better it would be for 'race relations'...Step by step racism was institutionalised, legitimised, and nationalised. (1984 p381)

The importance of immigration legislation in 1962, 1968 and 1971 sent a message to black people in Britain, that blackness and being British were incompatible. It would be in the arena of nationalism that the children of Caribbean migrants, born in Britain, would have to struggle to carve out their space in a hostile society.

Farrukh Dhondy was an ex-school teacher and later became the Commissioning Editor of Channel Four's Multicultural Programming.

One result of black anger with the education system was the setting up of Supplementary schools.

left: Darcus Howe addresses demo before it moves off.

right: Darcus Howe, broadcaster and founder of the Race Today Collective. He feels a strong optimism for black Britain compared to the early days.

## Brainwash education to make us the fools!

In education this new generation suffered and resisted an education system designed to keep the white working-class in their place. This system faced increasingly difficult issues concerning 'race' and achievement. In 1971 Bernard Coard published his landmark pamphlet, 'How the West Indian Child is Made Educationally Subnormal in the British School System' in which he argued that black children were labelled to fail and there was a need to move away from a Eurocentric curriculum.

This new generation of black children born in Britain developed what Farrukh Dhondy (1974 ) describes as a 'Culture of Resistance':

> They are a breed most dangerous to capital as they refuse to enter the productive partnership under the terms that this society lays down. They have turned the sale of their labour into a seller's market by refusing to do dirty jobs…School has not succeeded in inspiring them with ambitions they know they will not be allowed to fulfil. Their ambition can be characterised as survival. They refuse to work as their parents' generation did. They need very little convincing about the slavery of that process, they are the children of it. Their culture is a day to day affair, an affair of the styles and fashions they collectively generate. They educate themselves within the community, and carry their community into the school where one may see them gathered around reggae, developing the social image of their groups. (1974 p 49)

Dhondy points to school as the reproductive organ of a system designed to produce another generation of compliant workers, who would staff London Transport, the hospitals and the assembly line. The black explosion in schools during the late sixties and seventies saw these children resisting this process of socialisation. As Dhondy (1974) says:

Paul Boateng, now an MP, his Afro captures the spirit of the time.

They expected that the machine that had processed white labour power and passed it through the sieve of the meritocracy, would do the same for the Blacks. It didn't. The Black population, in two distinct steps, carried their opposition to the forms and functions of schooling through the cohesion of their communities into the schools. (1974 p46)

Some schools tried to respond to the problem by providing 'Black studies' programmes. This came out of political initiatives undertaken by some black parents alongside black nationalists e.g. The Hackney Black Parents Association. These programmes became a kind of 'special needs initiative' by schools and never touched the fundamental structural problems in the schooling process. As Dhondy (1974) says:

It is futile for a Black studies course to attempt to encapsulate their culture. Its only text is survival, and it is bound by a rejection of the disciplines of work that the society offers them, and can therefore be called a culture of resistance. It is a culture antithetical to the idea of schooling, and so finally unco-optable. (1974 p50)

It would be outside Britain that the forging of this new 'alternative' culture would seek inspiration. In this quest schools faced more than just resistance in the classroom but an ideological conflict.

Black youth saw the police as the problem.

77

## Chant down Babylon: the rise of Rasta

It was the adopting of the Rasta philosophy on life that helped many black youth in the 1970s to fight economic and psychological despair. As Hiro says:

> In the 1970s many young West Indians came to identify with Africa as the continent of their origin, in particular with the Ethiopia of Haile Selassie. This was the result of an amalgam of social, educational, psychological and economic factors. Hiro (1992: p82)

Even Hiro falls in the trap of calling Britain's first generation – 'West Indian' it would be a tag that the media would use to describe a group that was anti the norms of society. For working-class black youth Rasta offered an alternative to a society that still believed in the National Front slogan: 'There ain't no Black in the union Jack'. For the first time there was a spirituality that focused not on blue-eyed Jesus, but a God that identified with black people. This mental exodus back to Africa actually went via Jamaica, as did many things in the seventies. Rasta had taken off in Jamaica and it was the ideology that drove and shaped the new music called reggae. In other words for the first time black youth throughout the diaspora began to identify with one image and religion – which was based on race and nation. The power of Rastafari for Britain's new generation of black youth is summed up by Simon Jones:

> By the mid-1970s, the common currency of Rasta terminology and political concepts amongst young blacks was being signalled by the ubiquitous use of words and expressions such as 'seen', 'pressure', 'Babylon' and 'dread'. It was not surprising that concepts such as 'Babylon system' with its incisive critique of the systematic nature of capitalist oppression, should prove so widely relevant to young blacks, given the nature of their encounters with the state. The notion of 'Babylon' provided black youth with a critical tool with which to grasp the race and class mechanisms responsible for their subordination, while the discourses of 'truths and rights' and equal rights and justice' supplied a complimentary ideology of liberation which insisted on progressive and revolutionary change.

> The dynamics and conditions of racial oppression in the British context lent the politics of Rasta an added poignancy for young blacks, placing the movement's positive evaluation of blackness to the forefront of its appeal. Rasta's discourses of exile, estrangement and dispossession proved highly apt to the circumstances of blacks in Britain, while its notions of 'tribulation' and 'sufferation', founded on the specificity of black experience, provided a cultural bulwark against the racism of the dominant society. Jones (1988: p48)

This generation still had the Judaeo-Christian framework to understand how Rastafari was a wonderful reversal of what one learnt in Sunday school. A white blue-eyed Jesus was a lie – God was black and he was also the King of Ethiopia. For dub poet Linton Kwesi Johnson, though he believed Haile Selassie was no God, he shared the political commitment of the Rasta movement. Johnson, who was born in Jamaica but went to school in London, was by 1975 the key poetic voice of black Britain. He captured the rage and fire in the new generation of black British in what he called reggae poetry. Later he would team-up with Dennis Bovell and put his poetry under a drum and bass rhythm that made Linton a performance poet of the decade. His poem 'Yout Rebels' sums of the feeling of the seventies generation:

Linton Kwesi Johnson

This poem captures the dominant theme of movement in this book. It is the characteristic of Windrush generation and their children. In the face of colonialism and the new racisms in Britain, there was always a dynamic for change, for justice and creativity.

## Yout Rebels

*a bran new breed of blacks*
*have now emerged,*
*leadin on the rough scene,*
*breakin away*
*takin the day,*
*sayin to capital neva*
*movin forward hevva.*

*they can only be*
*new in age*
*but not in rage,*
*not needin*
*the soft and also*
*shallow councilin*
*of the soot-brained*
*sage in chain;*
*wreckin thin-shelled words*
*movin always forwud.*

*young blood*
*yout rebels*
*new shapes*
*shapin new*
*patterns creatin*
*new links*
*linkin*
*blood risin surely*
*carvin a new path*
*movin forwud to freedom*

## Black identity and the role of reggae

It was no coincidence that the intense resistance of black children in British schools occurred at the same time as black power uprisings in America and, more powerfully, the flourishing of the Rastafarian movement in Jamaica. These developments were all linked to an oppression based on race and class. The Rasta movement's influence increased steadily in Britain between 1970 and 1981, and its Pan-African, Ethiopianist ideology can be considered to have formed the core of a mass movement during the mid – seventies. It began in the 1930s in Jamaica when followers of the Pan-African leader Marcus Garvey developed a movement that sought to reverse the colonial cosmology around them. Central to this new ideology was the idea that God was black and Africa was their true home, to which they would one day return. This desire for a new home came from their spiritual and psychological alienation from the imitation-British Jamaican society. As Rex Nettleford (1970) puts it:

> To the Rastafarians who are black, Jamaica becomes the Babylon which holds them in the captivity of a protracted diaspora. Here there is no pleasure of exile, only oppression and suffering at the hands of imperialist Europeans and 'their derivatives' (meaning the Jamaican brown men and privileged evolved black members of the middle classes). There is, too, among the oppressed blacks a deepening of the conviction that the Return is imminent, that redemption and freedom for the true (black) Israelites is in the land of their forefathers – Africa in general and Ethiopia in particular. The Promised Land of Ethiopia awaits the Return (Repatriation) of the 'children of the seed of Israel' and the ruler Haile Selassie fulfils in the twentieth century the prophecy that a 'king would arise out of Jesse's root' as 'God Almighty for his people and a liberator of all the oppressed of the earth.' The oppressed of the earth are all black people whose forcible displacement (i.e. slavery) from their original habitat Ethiopia until this day, has caused the slaves to be resentful and at times revengeful of the cause of their enforced exile and ultimate privation. Nettleford (1970: p41–42)

During the 1970s black youth were able to find strength in a philosophy – Rasta, and a music – reggae, that the white mainstream did not understand and never took seriously. Reggae was considered to be unmarketable and unpopular in the music business. The narrow minded philistines complained that it sounded monotonous and failed to

DJ David Rodigan

Lovers Rock queen,
Carroll Thompson.

measure up to the standards of white pop. Derek Chinnery, former head of Radio One, summed up the BBC's position on reggae, arguing that:

It seems to be a regional interest, there doesn't seem to be much of a national demand for reggae...there's no strong indication that our listeners want more reggae. And, of course, there's an awful lot of reggae that's simply not suitable for Radio One. Some of them have strong political content while others are just poor quality records. Melody Maker (1976: p36)

Who would believe that come the mid-nineties reggae, rap and black dance music would be spearheading Radio One's schedule. The BBC had already banned Max Romeo's 'Wet Dream' for being too sexually suggestive. In 1969 and in 1979 Rupie Edward's song 'Irie Feeling' was banned because of its indirect reference to marijuana.

It was not until 1979 when DJ David Rodigan a white DJ who loved reggae began his show Roots Rockers on Capital radio, that reggae got any serious airtime on mainstream radio. Rodigan had based his show on Jamaica's Michael Campbell's Dread at the controls. It was a fascinating mix of jingles, interviews, news, version excursions and, of course, new releases. Rodigan did not dilute the music and appealed to both, black and white, he says:

'I don't believe in trying to dilute the musical format...Nor do I ever think 'Oh, that's a bit heavy, they might not understand that,' despite the fact that a lot of white people might think 'well what the hell does that mean'. Because the people that make the music know what it means; the black audience who may have been born and bred in this country but nevertheless feel an affiliation because of their blood, roots and culture to the music, they know what it means. Now the odd thing is that I didn't come from that kind of background, and yet I feel as closely affiliated to that as they do, and I Know there are lots of other white people who do as well.'

However it was Islands record and Chris Blackwell who were able to market this new music, pioneered by Bob Marley and the Wailers, to a white market. He did this by packaging his groups in the same way as the current rock artists of the day. The intense media interest that surrounded the Wailer's 1975 tour of Britain, together with escalating sales of *Natty Dread*, signalled Marley's commercial breakthrough to a mass white audience. On reflection one can see how certain stereotypes about Jamaica and reggae music were popularised to feed the need to have artists who were rebels. For the black audience in Britain, Marley and the Jamaican reggae tradition was more than just an image to kick against middle-class suburbia. Marley's lyrics spoke to the real situation facing the Black diaspora – these were redemption songs for the dispossessed.

The struggle with the canon that said 'white equals British' was an attempt to decolonise a mental slavery which threatened to render this new generation as lost souls without any identity. The moral outrage that motors this decolonisation process is best captured by Frantz Fanon (1963):

> ...In decolonisation, there is therefore the need of a complete calling in question of the colonial situation. If we wish to describe it precisely, we might find it in the well known words: 'The last shall be first and the first last.' Decolonisation is the putting into practice of this sentence. Fanon (1963: p36–37)

The identity struggle of African-Caribbean youths in the seventies was not a simple mimicking of the cultural expressions of the Caribbean; they used it to help re-make themselves in a culture that rejected their presence. Cornel West (1993) talks of this process as a quest for validation and recognition:

> This state of perpetual and inherited domination that diaspora (the spread of African culture and people throughout the world) Africans had at birth produced the modern black diaspora problematic of invisibility and namelessness. White supremacist practices – enacted under the auspices of the prestigious cultural authorities of the churches, print media, and scientific academics – promoted black inferiority and constituted the European background against which African diaspora struggles for identity, dignity (self-confidence, self-respect, self-esteem), and material resources took place. West (1993: p17)

Paul Gilroy (1992) outlines three tendencies in defining black British youth culture. First, it is a culture that has to reckon with its position within international networks. Therefore it is a diaspora culture with influences from America, the Caribbean and Africa. Second, it is a culture that has been created from diverse and contradictory elements, and third, it has evolved through various stages, linked in different ways to the pattern of capitalist development.

The response by black youths to this complex circumstance was to turn to the black nationalist ideas within Rastafari. It was an ideology that would reconstitute and unify new world black people. The word 'Babylon' became a popular term as a critique of white institutions and capitalism. Black people were seen as prodigal sons who had now returned to their culture. It was a text about redemption, and black people in Britain were perceived as innocent victims in the face of white oppression. It is in this context that, Mac an Ghaill's (1988) anti-school 'Rasta Heads' must be seen. These were an African-Caribbean group in his study school who regarded their world as superior and more 'relevant' than that of the school authorities:

> The Rasta Heads' visibility within the school was partly due to their generation of style. This included dress, hairstyle, posture, language and the wearing of Rastafari colours. The teachers had reacted against this, as it was perceived as a threat to their social control. There was a systematic attempt to prevent student identification with Rastafarianism. The wearing of dreadlocks, hats, Rasta badges or colours were banned. No distinction was made by the school authorities between those who identified with it spiritually and those for whom it was a more loose cultural association. (1988 p97)

The struggles of black youths during the 1970s was based on a realisation that school was mirroring the same racist discourse that operated outside. It was not only processing these boys to take the place of their unskilled parents, it had also denied them any cultural space in the national consciousness. Their adoption and adaptation of Caribbean and black American forms of cultural resistance led many to totally reject the schooling process. In this battle for minds the position of the 'Black community' was key in providing and reinforcing an alternative consciousness. This was another important point in Dhondy's (1974) article:

> They refuse the work that society allocates to them. School is their most immediate experience of state institution, if indeed it isn't borstal or jail. Their rejection of work is a rejection of the level to which schools have skilled them as labour power, and when the community feeds that rejection back into the school system, it becomes a rejection of the functions of schooling. Dhondy (1974: p50)

## Tender reggae: Lovers' Rock

The seventies were not just a simple copy of what happened in Jamaica – Rasta and reggae would soon filter down into a distinct British expression. The

## Young, Gifted and Black

*Young, gifted and black*
*Oh, what a lovely precious dream*
*To be young, gifted and black*
*Open your heart to what I mean*
*There's a whole wide world to know*
*Who are young, gifted and black*
*And that's a fact*
*Young, gifted and black*
*You mustn't fear because you are young*
*There's a world waiting for you*
*It is a thing that's just begun*
*When you feel really low*
*Yeah*

*There's a virtue you should know*
*To be young, gifted and black*
*You are so intact*
*Oh, young, gifted and black*
*Yes, oh I long to know the truth*
*Though at times when I was back*
*Then I was haunted by my youth*
*But what matters today is that*
*We can all cry out and say*
*To be young, gifted and black*
*Is where it's at*
*Young, gifted and black.*

Bob and Marcia

struggle to become a distinct cultural entity that is valued within white Britain and across the diaspora has been a tough struggle for black people in Britain and continues today. In a strange way the Caribbean was a mother that black people needed to let go in order to find themselves. At the heart of the seventies is a struggle to be taken seriously. The pressure of racism meant that being black and British was always problematic. It was often easier to become a pseudo-Jamaican. However, even this was not really satisfactory as the new generation began to realise it was a product of many influences.

In London those who identified more closely with black America called themselves Soul Heads. While others identified more closely with Jamaica and the philosophy of Rasta. The American influence was very important, not only in terms of style and music – see James Brown. It was the impact on television of Muhammad Ali, the great heavy-weight champion of the world, that really helped to focus the black community in Britain on the road to black Pride. In many ways it was a period when blackness came out of the closet. People were visibly asserting their 'black' identity.

Critics of the seventies suggest that it was a tough masculine era with no tenderness and interest outside of race politics. This is not true. The creation of Lovers rock, was not only an alternative to the roots reggae political message. It was a distinct black British sound. Lovers rock did many things it cut the divide between soul and reggae, it propelled a number of British female singers to stardom. The most popular being Janet Kay and Carroll Thompson. For the first time the sisters got a look-in even if it was a brief one and Janet Kay hit the pop charts with her tune *'Silly Games'*.

Janet Kay
below: Aswad was one of the first British reggae bands to take off, April 1976.

While expatriate Caribbean musicians had been living and performing in Britain since the 1950s, it was the emergence of a characteristically British genre of reggae music which began to speak of a new stage in the struggle for a promised land. A whole string of British groups, such as Misty, Aswad, Steel Pulse, Matumbi, the Reggae Regulars and Black Slate emerged in this period reflecting the growing political awareness and confidence of black youth. Songs like Steel Pulse's *'Handsworth Revolution'* and Delroy Washington's *'Streets of Ladbroke Grove'* and of course Matumbi's classic *'Empire Road'* – which also was the theme tune for one of Britain's first black sit-coms on television. The other classic was Tubby Cat Kelly's *'Don't call us no immigrants'* which sought to express the oppression and struggle in urban black life. Black Slate lead singer Keith Drummond explains:

You don't know what they're going through in Jamaica. You can only read it second-hand. So sing about the sufferation you're going through here…They say you can't make reggae unless you're a sufferer. Well, it's not just the Jamaicans who suffer. We suffer too, and now we're singing about our own condition. (Black Music, July 1977 p18)

The success of Lovers Rock was more than just a musical victory. It heralded a new confidence in black youth, who for the first time could let go of the apron-strings of Jamaica and stand alone. It finally put paid to the notion that the authentic version had to come from 'yard' or 'real' Jamaica. The image of 'movement' and a sense of feeling at 'home' are powerful in this context. It also heralded the movement of the 'muse' the goddess of inspiration had moved from Kingston, Jamaica and was resting in Handsworth, Tottenham and Brixton.

David Hinds of
Steel Pulse

Matumbi, a great British reggae band.

## Reggae Gone International

*Reggae dis a reggae*
*Dis a roots rock reggae*
*Reggae dis a reggae*

*Reggae gone international*
*Reggae gone multinational*

*Me say we mek it down in yard*
*And export it out abroad*
*Mix it down on tape*
*And transfer it to record*

*Reggae gone international*
*Reggae gone multinational*

*Well we make 45s and*
*We make Lps*
*Its a little sound*
*For you and me*

*Reggae gone international*
*Reggae gone multinational*

*Meh seh me hear it on radio*
*And see it on television*
*Hear it in America*
*And hear it in London*

*Reggae gone international*
*Reggae gone multinational*

*Reggae make you feel*
*Make you feel alright*
*Doesn't matter if you're black*
*If you're brown or if you're white*

*Reggae gone international*
*Reggae gone multinational*

*Well we started with ska*
*Then rock steady and now reggae*
*Ska and rock steady*
*Pave the way for the reggae*

*Reggae gone international*
*Reggae gone multinational*

*Me seh me hear it on Venus*
*And me hear it on Mars*
*Feel it in the sun*
*And the moon and the stars*

*Reggae gone international*
*Reggae gone multinational*

Mikey Dread

When he was king! Ali was an inspiration to many black people during the seventies.

## Conclusion

If Rastafarian philosophy was the content of this new movement, then its engine was reggae music. In the early 1970s it was the rise of singer Bob Marley that was significant in facilitating the popularisation of Rastafarian ideology in Britain and throughout the world. It gave reggae music a place in the lexicon of pop. Bob Marley's reggae was, like all reggae, a hybrid marked as much by its ties to American rhythm and blues as by its roots in Mento and calypso. One of the best known songs of Marley's middle period, *'Three O' Clock Road Block'*, for example, was extrapolated from Cole Porter's *'Don't Fence Me In.'* Paul Gilroy (1987) argues that it was not only the black communities that were influenced by Bob Marley; his music appeal was world-wide:

> If Marley's excursions into pop had been the ground for this two-tone harvest, this era suggests that the lasting significance of his rise to prominence lies not at the flamboyant extremities of youth sub-culture where punks had reworked the themes and preoccupation of Rastafari around their dissent from and critique of Britishness, but in the youth-cultural mainstream. Here, the posters of Bob, locks flying, which had been inserted into his crossover product by Island, became icons in the bedroom shrines of thousands of young whites. In his egalitarianism, Ethiopianism and anti-imperialism, his critique of law and of the types of work which were on offer, these young people found meanings with which to make sense of their lives in post-imperial Britain. Gilroy (1987: p171)

This is a key point. The impact of Jamaican music which was filtered through the black presence in Britain was not a cultural side-show. During the seventies it gave energy to the main core of youth sub-culture in Britain. The well known movements such as punk rock and the flourishing of white reggae bands such as UB40, Madness and Bad Manners hijacked the Jamaican music of the sixties. However, the most interesting phenomenon of this period was the cultural mixing and contextualising which took inspiration from the Caribbean and America and made it a distinctly black British expression. This meant that black youth cultures were developing around Britain and taking on the core problem of cultural definition and redefinition. However, for those born in Britain of Caribbean parents it was an everyday struggle of making a mark in a world that would leave you in its margins.

It would be during the 1980s and 1990s that the notions of 'the real black community' and 'positive images' would be seriously questioned. There would no longer be an uncontested consensus. The 'innocent' rhetoric around what constituted the black community could no longer apply. It is into this new context that many of the second and all of the third generation of African-Caribbeans find themselves.

# From Roots
# to Routes (1981
# and all that...)

previous page: Cleopatra mix and match in a style that has many black influences.

*The fundamental problem was, if I was going to continue to live in Britain, how was I to reconcile the contradiction of feeling British, While being constantly told in many subtle ways that I do not belong*

Caryl Phillips

*What is at issue here is the recognition of the extraordinary diversity of subjective positions, social experiences and cultural identities which compose the category 'black'; that is, the recognition that 'black' is essentially a politically and culturally constructed category, which cannot be grounded in a set of fixed transcultural or transcendental racial categories and which therefore has no guarantees in Nature*

Stuart Hall

*We were meant to rule the world*

Biggie Smalls

## THE ETHNIC COMPOSITION OF BRITAIN'S POPULATION, FROM THE 1991 CENSUS

| Ethnic group | No. | % |
|---|---|---|
| White | 51,873,794 | 94.5 |
| Black Caribbean | 499,964 | 0.9 |
| Black African | 212,362 | 0.4 |
| Black – other | 178,401 | 0.3 |
| Indian | 840,255 | 1.5 |
| Pakistani | 476,555 | 0.9 |
| Bangladeshi | 162,835 | 0.3 |
| Chinese | 156,938 | 0.3 |
| Other Asian | 197,534 | 0.4 |
| Other – other | 290,206 | 0.5 |
| **Total ethnic minority population** | **3,015,051** | **5.5** |
| Black ethnic groups | 890,727 | 1.6 |
| South Asian | 1,479,645 | 2.7 |
| Chinese and others | 644,678 | 1.2 |

# FROM ROOTS TO ROUTES (1981 and all that...)

The grandchildren of the Windrush generation begin their Exodus experience somewhere between the beginning of the eighties and the end of the nineties. The navigation for this generation is within the United Kingdom which is influenced by America and Europe. It is a journey within that seeks, not only ancestral identity but cross-cultural connections that make it hard to stick safely with the old categories of 'black' and 'white'. This is a time where identity is not as simple as black and white.

In looking back at those men who came off the Windrush in 1948 they were more than literally in the same boat as they began to face British racism. They certainly shared the same taste in fashion. Most wore trilbie hats, zoot suits and a look of vulnerability. The generation growing up at the end of the 20th century value their diversity – some follow the American influenced Nation of Islam, some are Christian. There are those who are middle or working-class. When it comes to politics there are a range of perspectives. In terms of values, beliefs and cultural style the black British communities are not an un-differentiated mass but complex and diverse.

This period begins in 1981 with two key events that act as a watershed for race relations in Britain and goes on to affect every institution in the land. The Brixton uprising and the New Cross massacre sent a clear signal to everyone in Britain: 'Deal with the racism and oppression faced by the Black communities or face protracted civil unrest'. Britain would never be the same.

The first half of the 1980s proved to be the most violent in British race relations history. The conflict was less to do (as it was in 1958) with white against black but white policemen against black communities. A number of factors went into what would be later known as the Brixton Uprising. First, black youth unemployment in 1980 had reached 55 per cent in some areas. Second, the police continued with their use of section 4 of the Vagrancy Act of 1824, which empowered them to arrest a person on suspicion of 'loitering with intent to commit an arrestable offence'. This was better known as the 'Sus' laws and it was used in a racially biased manner. The police bias was obvious from the fact that although African Caribbeans were only about 6 per cent of London's population, they accounted for 44 per cent of the total Sus arrests. In the London borough of Lambeth, covering Brixton, this figure rose to 77 per cent.

Another factor was that in January of 1981 a fire at 439 New Cross Road in Deptford, London, resulted in 13 young black people losing their lives. Many black people were convinced that the party was fire-bombed by white racists. This was opposed by police officers who said that no attack came from outside of the building. Given the lack of attention by the press and the police failure to look at the racial links to this tragedy – Britain witnessed one of the largest demonstrations of black political power. It took place on March 2, 1981. On that day 15-20,000 black people, under the banner of the New Cross Massacre Action Committee, demonstrated through the streets of London. The demonstrators were also protesting the lies, distortions and misreporting in the British press on issues arising out of the fires, as well as the failures of the Thatcher government to respond sensitively to the incident. According to political activist John La Rose:

left: America continues to have an influence on the cultural and religious landscape of Britain. The Nation of Islam has had a big influence on young black men in Britain.

below: 493 New Cross Road – scene of the fire!

> The major issue, which arose out of the New Cross Massacre, is still to be resolved. Who was responsible for setting fire to that house and how was the fire actually set? To this day these questions are still in the dark. It is much more than that though. The New Cross Massacre Action Committee had to exercise every ounce of alertness and vigilance to prevent the police from framing a group of young black people, who were at the party. La Rose (1984)

When asked about the relationship between the New Cross Massacre and what happened 3 months later in Brixton, he said:

> We crossed Blackfriars Bridge into the city. Blackfriars Bridge had not been crossed by a major demonstration since the Chartists in the 1830s. It marched down Fleet Street. It marched through the commercial centre of the city, Regent street, parallel to Oxford Street...For cynical reasons of state, a month after New Cross, Thatcher and the Queen had sent messages of condolence to the victims of a fire in Ireland in the constituency of the then Prime Minister, Charles Haughey. And they said ab-

below left: Black Peoples Day Of Action. One of the biggest demonstrations of black people in post-war Britain

below right: Demonstrators confront police on Black Peoples Day Of Action – 2nd March 1981

bottom right: The aftermath of the uprising in Brixton, London, April 1981

solutely nothing of the holocaust in London, the capital city of the country. For us it was an act of barbarism.

On the Friday evening of 10 April 1981, 19-year-old Michael Bailey from Brixton was snatched by his friends from the police as he bled from a stab wound. He was then taken to an ambulance. Rumours circled that Bailey had died at the hands of police. Despite this, the police continued with what they called 'Operation Swamp' by posting an extra 96 officers on Brixton streets on 11 April 1981. This policy was totally counter productive and ended in one of Britain's worst nights of violence. The incident sparked all that bottled-up anger that black youth had against the police. The rioting was vicious and intense. By nightfall Brixton was alight. The eruption was reported as far as Russia. It lasted two days and included the first use of petrol bombs on mainland Britain. At its peak about 7,000 officers were deployed to restore order in an area less than a square mile. This author remembers one officer from Yorkshire asking him the directions to Railton Road. The total damage amounted to £6.5 million.

The country was really shocked by the events, particularly the government who had not heeded any of the warnings. In April, Lord Scarman was appointed to 'inquire urgently into the serious disorder in Brixton'. Scarman reported on October 30, he said:

> Many of the young, particularly, but not exclusively the young of ethnic minority, had become indignant and resentful against the police, suspicious of everything they did…It produced the attitudes and beliefs which underlay the disturbances, providing the tinder ready to blaze into violence on the least provocation, fancied or real, offered by the police. Scarman (1981)

In 1985 a similar toughening up by the police in Brixton resulted once again in an outbreak of violence. The trigger to this incident followed the Police's handling of the shooting of Mrs Cherry Groce. A week later in Tottenham, North London, another police raid resulted in the death of a black mother Cynthia Jarrett. The violence the next day continued until midnight. During the violent exchanges PC Keith Blakelock was hacked to death. Winston Silcott was arrested for his murder, after a vicious press campaign, and he later won an appeal against a miscarriage of justice.

## The Aftermath

In 1987, the four major political parties fielded 29 black and Asian candidates. Keith Vaz, a Goan born in South Yemen, became Labour MP for Leicester East; Diane Abbott became the first black woman MP for Hackney North and Stoke Newington, Paul Boateng, a black barrister, won Brent South for Labour; and Bernie Grant became the Labour MP for Tottenham. In 1997 only one black MP who got elected and that was Oona King who won a seat in Bethnal Green. In terms of office the biggest appointment went to Bill Morris, the only black leader of a trade union was elected general secretary of the TGWU in 1992. Morris was earlier the leader of the Bus driver's Union, which was a key appointment given the link between black workers and London Transport.

Bernie Grant, Diane Abbot, Paul Boateng and Keith Vaz, elected as Labour MPs in June 1987.

There were many black gains in sport during this period. In 1993 Paul Ince became the first Black player to captain the England side in a match against the USA. Today, an estimated 25 per cent of professional footballers in England are black. Yet despite this domination on the pitch, few black people actually go to matches because of the overt racism and violence. It is still tough to play for England and find your own countrymen treating you with contempt. Racism at football grounds continues to be a problem with crowds chanting racial abuse at black players.

Winston Silcot. He was wrongly convicted of the murder of P.C. Blakelock, in a case of miscarriage of justice.

Bill Morris, the head of Britain's biggest Union the T&GWU. Once called the most powerful black man in Britain.

Cynthia Jarrett, her death sparked off the disturbances at Broadwater Farm.

## Playing for England

Lord Tebbit, when he was a Tory MP, once said that the test of black loyalty to Queen and country depended on whether you passed the 'Cricket' test. Put simply if you are genuinely English then you must support England. Playing for England means that you cannot have any affairs with a culture outside of Britain. You are not allowed to support the Caribbean and England at the same time.

In 1983 the Tories put-out an election poster, it was an image of a young black man, smartly dressed in a suit with wide lapels and flared trousers, the caption said: 'Labour says he's black. Tories says he's British'

These were two key examples that spoke clearly to black Communities that the Journey was far from complete. The Tory notion of 'One Nation' simply meant that you couldn't be black and British at the same time and being British was wearing a standard suit and tie. This attitude would inform all of Britain's key institutions, race was seen as irrelevant or impolite. However, racism continued, particularly racist attacks. It was the death of Stephen Lawrence in 1993 which re-focused Britain on the issue that race and racism still played a key part in how black people would see themselves in relation to the wider British society. What was significant about the murder of Stephen Lawrence was just how the police made a whole series of failures in terms of crime detection and the racist focus of the killing. Stephen and his friend had been waiting for a bus when Stephen was fatally stabbed in an attack by a number of white youths. The failure of the police to convict the known suspects was received with dismay by the whole nation.

## Giving Black Britain a 'Voice'

The aftermath of 1981 saw the birth of the Voice Newspaper, which went on to become Britain's best selling newspaper. The Voice took a significant departure from the existing Black press. Up to this time most of the papers were really keeping those from the Caribbean updated with news from home. Papers such as the *'Daily Gleaner'* and *'Caribbean Times'* catered for those who wanted news about the Caribbean. The Voice emphasised Britain. There was a new market of British born black people with little interest in the politics of the Caribbean but keen to follow the developments of the black community in Britain.

left: Black British confidence. Paul Ince, Liverpool and England. He likes to be known as the 'guvnor'.

right: Flying high! Footballer Ian Wright has proved to himself that he can make it in Britain.

The nineties (1998) saw the death of Enoch Powell and few black people had shed any tears. Enoch Powell was a senior Conservative minister before he was sacked by Edward Heath in 1968. Not, even the Tories could stomach his inflammatory speeches against Immigration. As a Euro-sceptic he left the Tories in 1974 over their pro-European policy. He then went on to join the Uster Unionists. In 1988 I wrote in the Sunday Mirror an obituary on Enoch Powell which read:

> Enoch Powell spent the last days before his death translating the New Testament from Greek to English. I wonder if he ever got to that bit which said 'Love thy neighbour as thyself.' For too many people Powell's legacy was one of hate not love.

Powell's rabble-rousing speech in Birmingham in 1968, with its images of foaming blood, overcrowded maternity wards, and impending

With the Conservatives, there are no 'blacks', no 'whites', just people.

Conservatives believe that treating minorities as equals encourages the majority to treat them as equals.

Yet the Labour Party aim to treat you as a 'special case', as a group all on your own.

Is setting you apart from the rest of society a sensible way to overcome racial prejudice and social inequality?

The question is, should we really divide the British people instead of uniting them?

**WHOSE PROMISES ARE YOU TO BELIEVE?**

When Labour were in government, they promised to repeal Immigration Acts passed in 1962 and 1971. Both promises were broken.

This time, they are promising to throw out the British Nationality Act, which gives full and equal citizenship to everyone permanently settled in Britain.

But how do the Conservatives' promises compare?

We said that we'd abolish the 'SUS' law.

We kept our promise.

We said we'd recruit more coloured policemen, get the police back into the community, and train them for a better understanding of your needs.

We kept our promise.

**PUTTING THE ECONOMY BACK ON ITS FEET.**

The Conservatives have always said that the only long term answer to our economic problems was to conquer inflation.

Inflation is now lower than it's been for over a decade, keeping all prices stable, with the price of food now hardly rising at all.

Meanwhile, many businesses throughout Britain are recovering, leading to thousands of new jobs.

Firstly, in our traditional industries, but just as importantly in new technology areas such as microelectronics.

In other words, the medicine is working.

Yet Labour want to change everything, and put us back to square one.

They intend to increase taxation. They intend to increase the National Debt.

They promise import and export controls.

Cast your mind back to the last Labour government. Labour's methods didn't work then.

They won't work now.

**A BETTER BRITAIN FOR ALL OF US.**

The Conservatives believe that everyone wants to work hard and be rewarded for it.

Those rewards will only come about by creating a mood of equal opportunity for everyone in Britain, regardless of their race, creed or colour.

The difference you're voting for is this:

To the Labour Party, you're a black person.

To the Conservatives, you're a British Citizen.

Vote Conservative, and you vote for a more equal, more prosperous Britain.

## LABOUR SAYS HE'S BLACK. TORIES SAY HE'S BRITISH.

**CONSERVATIVE ☒**

left: Conservative Party election poster, 1983.

above: Bernie Grant one of the first black MPs gets close to new MP Oona King.

national disaster – soon to be followed by icily calculated references to 'grinning piccaninnies' – mobilised and inspired popular racism all over the country.

In the same year Dockers and Smithfield porters downed tools and marched on the House of Commons in support of Powell. In the aftermath, a Jamaican had been shot and killed by a white gang armed with iron bars, axes and bottles; and crosses had been burnt outside black people's homes in Leamington Spa, Rugby, Coventry, Ilford, Plaistow, and Cricklewood. This marked a new feature in modern British social relations where an eminent politician inspired racist attacks and made hell of the daily lives of black and Asian people.

It was the Powell inspired Immigration Act of 1971 which virtually ended all primary immigration. Enormous power was put in the hands

Stephen Lawrence victim of racist attack.

of police and immigration officers: they could arrest suspected illegal immigrants without a warrant.

Historian Peter Fryer says: 'The black communities were now condemned by law to every kind of abuse, to harassment, detention without trial, separation of families, 'fishing raids' – to all manner of personal indignities, humiliations and sufferings, from the vaginal examination of women to find out if they were virgins…' He goes on: 'And again, as always, the legislative endorsement of racism, far from improving 'race relations', encouraged the fascists to step up their attacks.'

What is significant about the death of Enoch Powell is that it coincides with the 50th anniversary of the arrival of SS Windrush which brought the first significant migration of black people to Britain. Ironically it was a Tory health minister by the name of Enoch Powell who encouraged and welcomed this migration.

Edward Seaga                    Michael Manley

## The end of innocence and the new cultural hybridity

Music has been the key social/ cultural indicator for those in the African diaspora. It not only marks the mood or tempo of an age, but also acts as the major artery connecting African peoples across the globe. This was how the powerful ideology of Rastafari made its way into the hearts and minds of those in Africa and its diaspora. Therefore when 'the powerful march of Rastafari' (Gilroy 1987) ended, this was expressed in radical changes in the music. Gilroy reveals how the economic and political changes in Jamaica during the eighties had a dramatic influence on the music:

Michael Manley's socialist government in Jamaica was ousted by Edward Seaga's American-backed regime in 1980. This change had cataclysmic effects on the relationship between music and politics there, transforming both the content of the music and the structure of the music business. The largely Rasta-inspired singers, songwriters and dub poets who had guided the music to its place as a vibrant populist force for change in the society were brushed aside and their place taken by a legion of DJs or toasters. Manley's own path to a populist socialist politics had been guided by the semantics and vision of Rasta reggae, a fact he acknowledged in a discussion (1983) of Bob Marley's art, 'the greater part' of which he recognised as the 'language of revolution'. Under Seaga, the singers' and songwriters' influence faded and they retreated from the revolution which their Rasta language demanded. The DJs took centre stage. Gilroy (1987: p188)

In yer face! Yellowman

Edward Braithwaite (1985) summed up this new era by saying: 'Things have changed. Jamaicans no longer relate to that kind of nativeness.' One of the major characteristics of the Rastafari movement was its critique of capitalism, which saw the labour process as oppressive. It attacked the police and state for their militarism. There was a prevailing sentiment that freedom was a place where the poor would triumph over the rich. This was an inevitable historical process where the Rastaman would finally conquer this materialistic earth.

This critique was beset by a contradiction that would sow the seeds for its own decline. When the early Rastas first set up the movement, they were outcasts, but it was from this that they drew their strength. Babylon was down below in the changing 'madness' of Kingston while the Rastaman lived peacefully on the hills, living off the land and withdrawn from the Babylon system. The movement grew and became an urban development in the poor areas of Kingston, and took on a new dimension when reggae music became its most vital source of expression. The Rastaman (on behalf of a number of singers) became an international superstar. They had joined the capitalist market-place, with its emphasis on 'image' and its consumer-led orientation. Rastafarians' close links with the commodity – reggae music – meant that when this kind of music no longer sold the movement suffered a similar demise. The decline of radical reggae was seen by the shift from singers to DJs. The DJ was a kind of poet who spoke rhyming lyrics over the music bed of old reggae classics. What was the most controversial issue in this shift, was the contents of the DJ lyrics. They no longer proclaimed the Rasta ideals of social justice and black redemption in Africa; reggae's mainstay was gun machismo and black male sexual prowess. Gilroy (1987) illustrates this point when he describes the fortunes of 'Yellowman':

> The decline of radical reggae can be illustrated by reference to the career of Winston 'Yellowman' Foster, the most popular toaster of the early 1980s whose work took both Britain and Jamaica by storm during 1982. After two explicitly political sides chronicling the rise of authoritarian statism in Jamaica – 'Soldier Take Over' and 'Operation Eradication' – he opted for the safety of nursery rhyme, animal noises and anti-woman jive talk. (1987 p188)

*Say Cockney fire shooter. We bus' gun*
*Cockney say tea leaf. We say sticks man*
*You know dem have a wedge while we have corn*
*Say Cockney say 'Be first my son' we just say Gwaan!*
*Cockney say grass, we say outformer man...*
*Cockney say Old Bill we say dutty babylon...*

*Cockney say scarper we scatter*
*Cockney say rabbit we chatter*
*We say bleach Cockney knackered*
*Cockney say triffic we say wackaard*
*Cockney say blokes we say guys*
*Cockney say alright we say Ites!*
*We say pants Cockney say stride*
*Sweet as a nut...just level vibes. Seen.*

The Cockney Translator.
Smiley Culture.

103

This decline of a politically radical form of Jamaican music was replaced with a new sound that was less oppositional. At the same time black British music was ready to develop its own unique sound. With the Rasta canon in decline, the British scene was up for grabs. The language and politics of Rastafari had until this time blocked these new possibilities. There was a new confidence in this generation of black people who began to create a position for themselves in England. They soon began to redefine England and Britishness through a new a new idea of a multiracial Britain, in which they were here to stay. Whereas Rastafari had seen Britain as Babylon, the place of exile for the true sons of Africa, the new black British D.Js began to create a sense of belonging which went beyond the divisions of race and class. This was achieved through language. The trick was to create lyrics that drew from everywhere, it was an act of defiance, which refused to be confined by narrow categories. Gilroy(1987) points to the lyrics of DJ Smiley Culture in his 1984 hit record 'Cockney Translation'. He shows how this song presents a view of language as truly interchangeable; therefore what it means to be a Cockney has now changed for black youth. The song went into the pop charts and was popular with black and white youths, particularly in London.

The use of London black patois contrasted with cockney rhyming slang – showed that Black working-class youth were cockney by birth and experience but were denied this because of the way racism excluded them from the national character. The song also alludes to the hybrid or mixed nature of African Caribbean culture, which asserts a new kind of cultural politics. It defies the new racism and develops a political and cultural aesthetic that seeks to locate itself both as black and English.

## Raggamuffins in the Jungle

The Oxford Dictionary describes a Ragamuffin as a person in ragged, dirty clothes. It was this label (now spelled Raggamuffin) that Jamaican and black British youths would use from the mid-eighties to describe their culture. This was not a term of self-degradation, but was an identity that glorified in the raw side of manhood.

Again, the image was linked to music, this time led by DJs and had its African American version in what was earlier called Hip-hop but was later known as Rap music. The African diaspora influenced the black British context, as it had in the seventies. This time it was not a radical black nationalist political agenda that was passed through this medium but the red hot subjects of sex and violence. This caused controversy in black communities across the diaspora, and in some cases the State censored records. In Britain the black community have debated this new music intensely as parents worry about its influence on their sons. In his study of the cultural politics of race and nation in Britain, Paul Gilroy (1987) argues that:

> Jamaica's DJs steered the dancehall side of roots culture away from political and historical themes towards 'slackness': crude and often insulting wordplay pronouncing on sexuality and sexual antagonism. I am not suggesting a simple polarity in which all toasters (another word for DJs) were agents of reaction and all singers troubadours of revolution. The Jamaican DJ tradition had been involved in the spread of Rastafari during the late 1960s and early 1970s as recorded song...However the role and content of reggae changed markedly after 1980. (1987, p188 )

Yet, paradoxically, though DJ 'slackness' as critiqued by Gilroy is conceived as politically conservative, it can be seen to represent in part a radical, underground confrontation with the patriarchal gender ideology and the pious morality of fundamentalist Jamaican society. As well as a celebration of an aspect of black masculinity. In its invariant coupling with culture, slackness is potentially a politics of subversion. For slackness is not mere sexual looseness – though it certainly is that. Slackness is a metaphorical revolt against law and order; an undermining of consensual standards of decency. It is the antithesis of Culture. Carolyn Cooper (1993) supports this aspect of the DJ tradition:

> To quote Josey Wales: 'Slackness in di backyard hidin, hidin from Culture.' Slackness as an (h)ideology of escape from the authority of omniscient culture is negotiated in a coded language of evasive double-entendre. Gilroy (1990) himself notes, but does not fully explore at the level of politics, the subversive potential in the ability to switch between languages of oppressor and oppressed. (1993 p141)

This brings me back neatly to my point about Raggamuffin: the post-modern creative drive in the culture of the diaspora is to subvert the oppressors' text/language by making it your own. Raggamuffin, or its shortened version Ragga, no longer means a man with dirty clothes, it is an assertion of self by shifting or subverting the cultural margins.

The development of Ragga music from Jamaica and the African American expression of Rap music, although different styles of music, have been the most powerful influences on the landscape of black British culture during the 1980s and 1990s. Its most powerful detractors have been twofold: First, a political criticism that sees Ragga and Rap as displacing the political energies that were found in older black cultural expressions, like the Blues or Rastafari. The second is a feminist critique which sees Rap as misogynist and glorifying a black sexism.

Greg Tate (1993) recognises the hugely expanded forum that Rap (or Hip-hop) music, as a popular form, has made possible. At the same time, he is frustrated by the commercial dictates and by the ever more exacting decrees of style politics:

> A lifetime of Tarzan and John Wayne teaches us that when the drums fall silent, the pink man should really begin to know fear. Conventional wisdom would have us believe that Hip-hop predicted all but the day and time of the Los Angles rebellion. But what if Hip-hop is not the expression of Black folks' rage, but only another momentary containment of it, or worse, an entertaining displacement? During the Gulf conflict, hip-hop's drums were deafeningly silent. They went on to the beat of cash registers while the F-15s were taking out Baghdad's mothers and children until the break of dawn…Cornel West has called Rap visionless, but what it is, even at its most progressive, is agendaless. It reacts better than it proposes, and we who feebly wait for Hip-hop nationalists to salve our rage and pain, hoping they will speak with us or for us, are to blame for not developing our own ways to radically speak above the fray. Hip-hop should be an invitation for everyone to break the silence around injustice, but it has become an invitation to party for the right to demagoguery. As a successful counter-cultural industry, whose style assaults have boosted the profits of the record, radio, junk food, fashion and electronic industries, Hip-hop's work is done. But as a harbinger of the black revolution, Hip-hop has yet to prove itself capable of inspiring action towards bona-fide social change. Now we'll see, like Bob Marley sang, who's the real revolutionary. After all, real bad boys move in silence. (1994 p1)

One act that tried to be more than just a servant to the record industry was Soul II Soul, the huge black and style collective that took London by storm during the mid -eighties. At the core of their Funki-Dred style is a commentary about where black culture has arrived since the Windrush. Their music/style are anthems to the diaspora. American Funk meets Jamaican Dread/Reggae through black Londoners. According to the founder and co-ordinator of the project, Jazzie B:

> 'I went to school with people from many different nationalities and religions – from Greeks to Asians to Jews, from Jews to Muslims, from Muslims to Catholics to Rastafarians.

> Our music could only have happened in Britain at that particular time, when everyone was naive and susceptible to almost anything that was going on. It was definitely, without doubt, a British thing. Growing up in the 1970s we were exposed to so many different styles. The

left: Keep on Moving, Jazzi B of Soul II Soul.

right: Boxer Lennox Lewis could be described as Mr diaspora, he was born in London of Jamaican parents and was raised in Canada.

foundation was reggae, but I listened to everything from Eddy Grant and the Equals to David Bowie and punk. We just moved with whatever was moving us at that time. The fact that we were brought up in Britain, with that mix of cultures, meant we took a little bit of everything and blended it in with our own style.

Our roots are very important but when we delve back into them, things are more complex, I go back to the Caribbean and they call me English, and yet when I am here in Britain I might be told to go back to my own country. So what is black British? To be honest I'm as British as the Union Jack.'

It is not only in music that we see this mixing and blending, we also discover it in the post – eighties fashion and hairstyles. In the seventies the Afro was popular as a signifier of pride, one had to hold one's head up to wear it. It was the sign of black pride. In Jamaica and London a similar statement was being made with dreadlocks. What both styles have in common is their claim to a 'natural' state or condition of Blackness. Those who wore these styles would say that they had kept their natural hair, as opposed to those who straightened or 'pressed' their hair.

In fact, all black hairstyles are cultivated – none are natural, the use of the Afro-pick to guide your hair in a certain direction, if it is an Afro, is far from natural. It is artificial and has nothing to do with a natural cultivation. The same can be said about dreadlocks. One of the pains of the seventies and early eighties was how some black people made claims about hair that would want to diminish others. It means that from weaves, curly perms to dreadlocks, no one has the upperhand.

Once we learn that there is nothing natural or innocent about black hair, we should be able to accommodate the diverse tastes. This generation must be seen as navigators of their own notions of identity across national boundaries to connect with the rest of the black diaspora across the world. In relation to the Windrush, which came in 1948, we see a return to those styles in some phases of youth culture. Those suits were just too good to be left alone in the 'grips' of the men in the Windrush, they have been raided in the eighties and nineties by a popular culture hungry for new ideas even though they have borrowed from the past.

Les Back (1996) gives three examples from young people about their attitude to having a British identity. Lorna is 16 years old. Of the ambiguous relationship between nationality and race, she says:

> 'If you identify yourself as a black person coming – with West Indian parents. It's like we – they like know they are coming from elsewhere. A lot of people don't see themselves as English. I think you should be aware of that. It is the way the country puts them down already. It makes you feel like you don't want to be from here. It's like when times are good, us – the people who are born here – are considered English, just like everybody else. But when things are bad, jobs are hard to get, we become black!'

It is this tenuous and fragile sense of belonging and feeling excluded which is captured in the above quote. There is something problematic about being black and English and the two are seen to be mutually exclusive.

Another group might vacate a notion of Englishness but still want to maintain their right to British citizenship. Jenny 15 says:

> 'Well I am British, I was born in London, but I am not the same as the English people, it's like I am a different kind of English – a different way. I mean we have different ways – a different culture. But I am still British.'

The key line here is a 'different kind of English'. For the first time the new dynamic in black culture will make a distinction between being British as a citizen in the legal sense of the word and having an English culture which is different than other expressions.

However, there were those who didn't see themselves British at all, they felt that being black gave them a status that was so special they could never be part of anything that called itself British. Geoff says:

> 'Well to me now I would define myself as a Black person. British, I would take that as an insult. No, I see myself as a black person of West Indian parentage. I don't want to be classified on the British side. I mean – no offence – but there isn't much to attract me to it.'

Maxi Priest and Apache Indian

The tension with British identity would continue throughout the Thatcher era which began in 1979. What was also happening at this time was a breakdown in the old certainties of British identity. Britain would have to try and define itself in relation to Europe. This would in the long run help to collapse the Conservative party as Euro-sceptics fought against the end of the so called 'British way of life' which John Major described as eloquently as young maids riding bicycles and the drinking of warm beer. British identity was now up for grabs and the name of the game was called 'pick and mix'. The eighties and the nineties were periods of uncertainty for all when it came to cultural, gender and racial identity. Ironically, it allowed for greater cross-fertilisation of cultures as groups began to feel open enough to borrow from each other.

This development had its most creative expressions in two musical forms – Bhangra with its mixture of traditional punjabi music with a dance beat and Jungle music. It was really in England that for the first time the Caribbean and Asian traditions would mix. In fact soon there were Bhangra mixes that had a ragga feel. The two best exponents of this combination was Maxi Priest and Apache Indian. During the promotion for '*Fe Real*', Maxi Priest and Apache Indian were the key stars at a Dilvali festival in Leicester. The Indians in Leicester mainly came from East Africa and some were thrown-out by Idi

Amin, black people in the area often complained about the hostile attitude that some in the Asian community have for African people. This concert would deliver a blow to this prejudice and show how modern Asian culture was being transformed by the children of the Windrush. Apache remembers the significance of the show:

> 'It was a nice warm kind of evening. They had 8,000 Asian kids on the streets. We never realised it was going to be that big. When we went on stage Maxi did his Indian (Punjabi) chorus, when they saw him singing that, it meant so much. The Maxi Priest thing was a huge thing, it is all to do with us being a very self- contained people and thinking don't know what is happening. They see a black person wanting to use the language. Then it is like Maxi Priest is an international star singing in Punjabi and then the Asian youth check it as – yeah people do want to know us. It was special.'

The era is often praised by sociologists as the shift from roots to routes. The sense that the cultural journey is no longer an ancestral one back to Jamaica, or even Africa, but it is movement across boundaries that are only a block away. It is making connections with friends and peers who may have different ancestries but have a unique local experience which becomes a fusion of many cultures. This has been tainted with the dogged persistence of racism and racist attacks. The murder of Stephen Lawrence at an Eltham, south London, bus stop is a constant reminder that the journey to the promised land continues full steam ahead.

The big questions that the new generation are asking relate to social mobility. How can the system deliver better opportunities, particularly in employment. In 1990 the Voice newspaper conducted its own survey of black aspiration. There was a mixed response to those oppressive structures which were identified. There were basically three categories.

The first and the most disaffected expressed hostility to integration of any sort. This was shown in a refusal to adopt mainstream British cultural practices. There was a strong identification with their parents or grandparents culture. There was a real resentment against the normal routes to social mobility such as education. This group tended to be poor or unemployed. An unemployed interviewee commented:

> 'I don't accept you can help me. Education is a waste of time. I am Black. The police hate me because I am Black. I am not British and never will be.'

The second group acknowledges that racism is an everyday part of their lives, but would not suggest that it was so bad that it was impossible to make gains in the society. This involves an identification with the culture of being 'black

Black women have enjoyed greater experimentation with hairstyles.

British', whilst also at the same time acknowledging that there are other ties on your loyalty and sense of self. One interviewee described it as living in two worlds and not being accepted in either. This produces a deep sense of unease:

'It took me a long time to work out what I am. It did, honestly it did. I was born and bred in Britain. But I got a nasty shock when I was not treated the same as everyone else. Now I identify myself as black British. I was born in Britain, but I am black of African descent and Caribbean origin. But I can't say I am Jamaican. Just a few years ago on my first visit to Jamaica I felt a sense of belonging, but it wasn't a deep-rooted thing. In Britain, I don't feel I belong. It's like I'm an alien. I have to live two lives.'

Ben Okri, winner of the Booker Prize for literature.

This position does not represent an absolute rejection of 'British' society and its values. It does not identify society as irremediably racist. However, it points to the strong ambivalence there still remains for black people on how to be reconciled to a national identity that still embodies racism.

The third group felt that black people can achieve social mobility and societal success, and though it is more difficult to ascend the ladder of educational opportunity, it is still possible and worthwhile. These respondents see themselves within the wider scope of the society and profess no meaningful ties with the Caribbean or Africa. If they talk of identity in racial terms they simply see themselves as 'black'. They are likely to have achieved success in the education system and they may be enjoying high socio-economic status.

All of the respondents found that even though they were second and third generation, their parents and grandparents culture still had a powerful influence on their lifestyle. This culture acts as a protection against the incomprehension, indifference and hostility from white people about their culture and background. In common with Vince Reid, who was 13 when he came on the Windrush, their school experience in particular remains the one where they feel white society just hasn't got a clue. An account of an interviewee's school experiences includes an example of this incomprehension:

It was a day we came in from games, and we were all wet. In the Caribbean community growing up, it's cultural to braid your hair. Now a couple of the girls in the class came in and their hair was wet, and with our texture hair, if it's out and it gets wet it goes frizzy, and it frizzes to the extent that it looks as if it's shrunk. So to prevent that happening the girls were just braiding their hair to keep it stretched. Now a couple of girls were doing that and the teacher walked in while this was going on and she said, 'Oh, you'd better stop that now. You're not in the jungle now'. We were angry. We were upset, but weren't articulate enough to be able to say anything back to her, to turn the insult round. But we explained why we were doing this, and we said that braiding actually stretches the hair or even pressing can stretch the hair. Pressing is when you use a hot comb and just comb it through your hair. She didn't realise that or she chose not to understand that point, and she said, 'Oh, how do you press your hair then, do you put your head down on an ironing-board, and get the iron and run it up.' This was what she said and you could see that she just didn't have a clue about our culture or anything about us, and this was the sort of person who was teaching us.'

The eighties and beyond is still known as the struggle for black children's minds and bodies in an education system fails to recognise their racial and/or cultural identities, and which also continues to exclude a disproportionate number of black boys from school.

## No where better than yard?

One of the historical ironies for the Windrush generation living at the turn of the century is their relationship to the Caribbean they left fifty years ago. They regularly support the economies back home. In the case of Jamaica, they represented in the nineties, the second biggest source of foreign currency. Some have decided to return home for good. Others have felt that they have been in Britain too long and they have all their family around them, so going back is not an option. The decision about going back can raise new issues about culture and identity. To what extent do these people feel 'English' or 'Caribbean'? How do you relate to a society that has dramatically changed since you left it? These are tough questions that have often split families as they struggle to find the most comfortable place for retirement.

This search to find a 'cultural space' dominated the ideas of author Victor Headley. Even though he is a British-born first generation writer. His main struggle becomes one of finding an 'authentic' culture. If things British are so negative, it is easier to find authenticity for 'self' and your lifestyle in Jamaica. His book 'Yardie', published in 1992 by X-press publishing, a black publishing house, led by journalists, Steve Pope and Doton Adebayo, struggles with these ideas.

Headley is known to be a man of few words and as one of the blessed few given the opportunity to interview him, he once said: 'Yardie will be remembered in years to come as the book which got black people into book shops in large numbers.'

This is a big claim for a novel so small but in many ways, to the annoyance of the black literati, it is true. The so-called popular novel had been written. Samuel Selvon's 'Lonely Londoners' is a wonderful tale, but this was still the musing of the Caribbean migrant. What we needed was a story based in England with grit, passion, controversy and lots of guns.

It did, 'kind of' come with 'Yardie' the story of D, the Jamaican cocaine courier who comes to Britain. He double crosses his supplier and sets himself up as a

Victor Headley,
the author of
Yardie.

gang leader. The story does not have anything more than this, making it a flimsy tale. His sojourn through the underworld of Harlesden, Ladbroke Grove and Hackney is where the book should have been strong. Instead, we get very bland descriptions of settings that needed a more detailed eye. When D first sees Hackney, Headley short changes us:

> On the landings of the block of flats, D could see and hear the residents' daily life unfold. Neighbours chatting, women chasing little children to get them home; usual everyday scenes in Hackney. The dwellings didn't look new and he stairways and corridors were far from clean but it was a long way from certain areas of West Kingston. This is what people called a 'poor' area in England, D reflected. It wasn't that bad.

This is a key passage in the book. We do not get an insight into Hackney because D and the author are mentally in Jamaica. Headley wants to give us a black British story but he can't pull himself from his own identity crisis. He is a black Brit that wants to be Jamaican. It reminds me of the days in the seventies when you went into a record shop and unless a record was stamped Kingston, Jamaica, then it wasn't authentic. Black British was considered second rate. This is a novel that indirectly gives us an insight into authenticity – particularly for the identity of the black British male. As D reflects he is able to dismiss Hackney as a soft option 'it wasn't that bad'. This has two meanings, Hackney or London is 'softer' in terms of its socio-economic infrastructure compared to the Jamaican ghetto but it also means that Jamaica has the 'authentic' gangster the real 'bad bwoy'.

This dualism of feeling left out of the mainstream of Britain and looking towards Jamaica as an authenticating force for your masculinity, has been a key driving force in black male expression. What Headley struggles with through D is the release of the black British self – whatever that may be. It is because this species is so uncertain – he can never make him his hero.

The novel is not really about first or second generation black Britons but newly arrived Jamaicans fighting it out on London streets. In this regard we had to wait until Diran Adebayo's 'Some Kind of Black' appeared to keep us rooted in the 'real' British experience. The term 'Yardie' was originally used by Jamaicans to differentiate between those that had been born in Jamaica, as opposed to those who were British born. Its meaning changed and took on the description of Jamaican gangsters.

The strength of Yardie lies in its pace and its context. We simply never had that this fascinating gangster lifestyle put into a book since Michael Thelwell's 'The Harder They Come'. Yardies had already been built up by the Sunday magazines to be the more brutal than the Mafia. However this was always some white middle-class guy on the features desk trying to translate the madness of

West Kingston, Jamaica, to those who lived in Kingston-Upon-Thames. Victor Headly had enough street cred to re-create this mysterious underworld. As the Daily Express put it: 'Headley is one of the first black authors in the country to write about the street from the street. He is not a lyrical stylist like Booker-Prize winner Ben Okri and nor has he had the plaudits of the literary establishment.

The novel did break ranks with a safe black middle-class literati that just wanted 'positive images'. Black Britain at the turn of the century is a highly literate generation and the popularity of the black novel is unprecedented both amongst black and white people. There may not be for some time a great novel about the Black British experience but at least we are developing a generation of readers and writers who want to read about their experience. American prize winning novelist Toni Morrison (1983) says:

> For a long time, the art form that was healing black people was music. That music is no longer exclusively ours; we don't have exclusive rights to it. Other people sing and play it, it is the mode of contemporary music everywhere. So another from has to take its place, and it seems to me that the novel is needed...now in a way that it was not needed before. Morrison (1983)

## Blackness goes to market

The publication of 'Yardie' raises the issue of the commercialisation of black culture. Can there be such a thing as authentic black culture when the industry that produces it is controlled by white-owned corporations? Black music and style have come to dominate the language of popular fashion. Black celebrities like athletes Linford Christie and model Naomi Campbell have now become key figures in promoting fashion. However, the corporate world still buys into stereotypes of black people which associate them only with the 'body' and not the mind. This isn't new when Chris Blackwell sold Bob Marley and the Wailers to the white world – he didn't use that famous picture of him as a family man behind a pram with Rita and the children, instead it was Marley in a haze of ganja – mystic and of course sexually available. White and to a certain extent black corporations have been clever in appropriating black style in order to sell a product. Black people are now firmly part of the commercial world. However, the joining-up fee should never cost black people their souls. On the other hand many in Britain have lost the confidence to enter the commercial world and so fail to multiply their talents.

In his book with bell hooks, 'Breaking Bread,' Cornel West defines a 'race transcending prophet' as 'someone who never forgets about the significance of race but refuses to be confined to race'. (1991) p49. Surely this should be the next port of call on our journey to the promised land.

Keep on dancing! Dancers
from the Northern School of
Contemporary Dance.

KANGOL®

## Conclusion

Professor Rex Nettleford of the University of the West Indies wrote a book called *'Inward Stretch, Outward Reach'*. I like the image conjured up by this title. It speaks of movement – not being static while the world moves on. This was really the vision of that great Jamaican leader Marcus Garvey who in the 1920s, without the help of radio, satellite television or a world-wide news agency used his newspapers, especially the *'Negro World'* to rally the black masses. His movement sought to educate black people world-wide about self-worth, creative potential and to frighten the colonial powers to release power to black nations worldwide. It was a remarkable vision, which may not have succeeded at the time but leave us today asking similar questions. Black people in Britain are a long way off controlling their own destiny in terms of education, business and culture. We play for teams but we don't own them.

The image of stretching inside yourself is about ambition, vision and consciousness. Those people who left on the Windrush, left their homes for a variety of reasons but I think Sam King summed it up well when he said: 'The reason why I left Jamaica was because I didn't want my children growing up in a colony'. The outward reach to Britain was another story. What was once the land of opportunity became a land of hostility and resentment.

One of the problems with outward reach is that you're likely to get your hand bitten off. What we must celebrate is that persistence not to be either a European clone or in some instances a copy-cat of America and the Caribbean. This means an inward stretch that does find your African ancestry but it also means reaching to other cultures and inspirations. As they say in Jamaica 'we reach!'

However, there's another stretching and reaching that not enough of the Windward generation have found time to do. It is 'reaching' the next generations of Black youth, who still suffer at the bottom of most social and economic indexes. They need to know the story of the Caribbean and the journey to a new life. They need to know how they fit into this legacy. They need to understand the pathways, both cultural and spiritual, that lead to them. Like the relay race, I hope this book has been a baton of experience to inspire the next generation.

left: Linford Christie OBE,
his physique is in demend.

# References

Berry, J. (1979) *Fractured Circles*, London, New Beacon Books

Brathwaite, E. (1967) 'The Emigrants' in *Rights of Passage*. Oxford University Press.

Bryan, B. Dadzie, S. Scafe, S (1985) *The Heart of the Race: Black women's lives in Britain*. London, Virago

Cooper, C. (1983) *Noises in the Blood: Orality, gender and the 'vulgar' body of Jamaican popular culture*. London Macmillan

Department of Archives Barbados (1950) *'Information Booklet for Intending Emigrants to Britain'*

Dhondy, F. (1978) *The Black Explosion in British schools*. Race Today Feb, pp44–7

Donald J. and A. Rattansi (1992) (eds) *'Race', Culture and Difference*. London, Sage.

Fanon, F. (1963) *The Wretched of the Earth*. New York, Grove

Fryer, P. (1984) *Staying Power: The history of black people in Britain*. London, Pluto Press.

Gilroy, P. (1987) *There Ain't No Black in the Union Jack: The cultural politics of race and nation*. London, Routledge.

Gilroy, P. (1992) 'The end of anti-racism', in J. Donald and A. Rattansi (eds), *op. cit.*

Gilroy, P. (1993a) *Small Acts: Thoughts on the politics of black cultures*. London, Serpents Tail.

Gilroy, P. (1993b) *The Black Atlantic: Modernity and double consciousness*. London, Verso

Hall, S. (1990) 'Cultural Identity and diaspora'. In J. Rutherford (ed) *Identity, Community, Culture, Difference*. London, Lawrence & Wishart.

Hall, S. (1991) *Old and new identities, Old and New Ethnicities*. In A.D. King (ed) *Culture Globalization and the World System*. Hampshire, Macmillan.

Hall, S. (1992) 'New ethnicities', in J. Donald & A. Rattansi (eds), *op. cit.*

Harpin, L. (1994) 'Jungle', *The Face* (No 71 August 1994) London.

Harris, P (1994) 'Out of the jungle', *The Voice* issue 456 July 1994 London, Voice Communications.

Hebidge, D. (1982) *Subculture: The meaning of Style*. London, Routledge.

Hebidge, D. (1988) *Hiding in the light: On the Images and Things*. London, Routledge.

Hiro, D. (1992) *Black British, White British*. London, Paladin hooks, B. (1993) *Hard-core rap lyrics stir backlash*. New York Times, August 15, New York.

hooks, B. (1994a) *Outlaw Culture, resisting representations*. London, Routledge.

Jones, S. (1988) *Black cultue, White youth: The reggae tradition from JA to UK* Hampshire, Macmillan

La Rose J. (1984) *The New Cross Massacre Story*. (Interviews with John La Rose) London, Race Today Collective.

Mac an Ghaill, M. ( 1988) *Young, Gifted and Black: Student – Teacher Relations in the Schooling of Black Youth*. Milton Keynes, OUP

Mullard, C. (1982) 'Multiracial education in Britain: from assimilation to cultural pluralism', in Tierney, J. (ed) *Race, Migration and Schooling*. London, Holt, Rinehart and Winston.

Nettleford, R. (ed) (1971) *Manley and the new Jamaica (selected speeches and writings 1938-1968)* Longman Caribbean.

Nettleford, R. (1993) *Inward stretch outward reach*. Macmillan Caribbean

Phillips, C. (1987) *The European Tribe*. London, Faber and Faber

Pilkington, E. ( 1988) *Beyond the mother country (West Indians and the Notting Hill white riots)* London, I.B. Tauris & Co Ltd

Tate, G. (1994) 'Introduction' in A. Ross and T. Rose 9 (eds) *Microphone Friends: Youth music, Youth culture*. London, Routeledge

Scarman, Lord. *The Brixton Disordres 10–12 April 1981*. Pelican Books Harmodsworth 1982

Sewell, T. *Sunday Mirror Column*. Feb 15 1998

West, C. (1993) 'The New Cultural Politics of Difference', In C. McCarthy and W. Crichlow (eds) *Race Identity and Representation in Education*. London Routledge.

# Index